The Glitter Effect

Copyright © 2018

Jacy Lee Pulford

ALL RIGHTS RESERVED

No portion of this publication may be reproduced, stored in any electronic system, or transmitted in any form or by any means, electronic, mechanical, photocopy, recording, or otherwise, without written permission from the author. Brief quotations may be used in literary reviews or for social media promotional or marketing.

All Scripture quotations are taken from the King James Version of the Bible unless otherwise indicated.

Cover art by author

www.helloawesome.live

To Jonathan:

You're my best friend and the love of my life. I couldn't have done this without your continual encouragement and support. Thank you for everything. I love you!

To David and Samuel:

God knew what He was doing when He created the two of you! I am a better person because I'm your mama. I'll do my best to guide you to the Lord as He continually works in my heart. Here's to a rich legacy in Jesus.

The Glitter Effect

Jacy Lee Pulford

Chapter 1: Glitter

Chapter 2: Shrapnel

Chapter 3: Foundations

Chapter 4: Trees

Chapter 5: Sinkholes

Chapter 6: Well Water

Chapter 7: Crossfire

Chapter 8: Good Fruit

Chapter 9: Reflection

Chapter 10: Pillars

1

Glitter

"God is powerful, but we still need to be purposeful."

Amber Mills Lia, Triggers

From the moment a baby is born, they search for guidance and direction. As their food instincts develop, we are to show them the way to nourishment. We are given the responsibility to show them where to be fed. Looking at this example with spiritual eyes, we have been given an opportunity to shine a light so that others can see Him through us. When young believers need guidance and direction, we are to usher them to the truth. We can be an influence of positive proportions.

"Let your light so shine before men, that they may see your good works, and glorify your Father which is in heaven."
(Matthew 5:16)

This world is changing fast every day. And the church is changing with it, both positively and negatively. Change can be beautiful and groundbreaking. Change can also be scary and confusing. *When change unfolds, it creates a ripple.* One thing we can always count on is that God doesn't change. We can trust in Him and the plans He has for us.

"I am Alpha and Omega, the beginning and the ending, saith the Lord, which is, and which was, and which is to come, the Almighty." (Revelation 1:8)

God's design for this life is pretty magnificent. Relationships are very important to the Lord. One life can weave into another life and create an impression. How we operate within the relationships we're in is vital to our growth as a person and the influence we have. God created us in such a way that we will influence other people around us. *There is power in our influence.* We can speak words that build or break. We can whisper love or fear. We can forgive or harbor hate. Influence is a gift or a curse and many of us are not aware of that power. In this modern world, the focus has been more on instant gratification and self-fulfillment. *And God weeps.*

We were never meant to thrive alone but alone we must be in the Throne Room.

It's crucial to our earthly survival to understand the impact our choices can make. Since there is power of influence through our choices, we must spend quiet time with God to make sure we are aligned with Him. When we spend time with God and He opens our eyes, it is then something amazing happens! We get a choice. *A choice!* Part of God's design is allowing us the free will to choose. The Creator of the heavens and the earth made it so when we were faced with a decision to follow ourselves or to follow Him, we could make that choice. It wasn't forced on us. This shows how loving God truly is. He is not a dictator but a merciful Father.

"For God, who commanded the light to shine out of darkness, hath shined in our hearts, to give the light of the knowledge of the glory of God in the face of Jesus Christ. But we have this treasure in earthen vessels, that the excellency of the power may be of God, and not of us. We are troubled on every side, yet not distressed; we are perplexed, but not in despair; Persecuted, but not forsaken;

cast down, but not destroyed; Always bearing about in the body the dying of the Lord Jesus, that the life also of Jesus might be made manifest in our body."
(2 Corinthians 4:6-10)

In those quiet moments with God, He will reveal to us things that must change. This not only is for our benefit and to strengthen our relationship with God, but also the relationships we have with others. When we are looking at our sins, it can be daunting. No one wants to see how sinful they are. It would be nice to pretend as if no problems exist at all, right? We want to put up a defense to somehow protect us from unpleasant emotions. We don't want to feel bad - about anything.

Luckily, the plan God created includes deliverance. After He has revealed to us our shortcoming, the most crucial step that comes next is repentance. It's a wonderful tool used to shape us - to mold us - into the people God knows we can be. Why? *Because everything is made to glorify the Lord, even our suffering.* He is glorified through our redemption. When the Lord Jesus Christ changes us, then we really can shine a light in this dark world!

"Every way of a man is right in his own eyes: but the Lord pondereth the hearts." (Proverbs 21:2)

It's important that I stand for the truth. The truth will guide me as I interact with my husband and our two sons. Following the truth God has shown me means I'm willing to look past my own pride to see the reality of my influence and the path God has set before me. If I don't seek the Lord's provision for my life and ignore the prompting to draw closer to Him, I'm not the only one who will be affected.

There's a lie that there are good people vs bad people.

The more God reveals Himself to me, the less I believe this to be fact. However, there is proof throughout scripture that there is a difference between good and bad *choices*. Every person is capable of both. The Bible provides real examples of people who were the dirtiest of sinners. *That is, until they turned to God and were changed.* It gives me hope! It doesn't matter how deep I am in sin, He is still available. Jesus is a Way Maker!

When I came to the Lord and moved into my first apartment, I had a hard time living alone. But the most important thing I learned is that spending time alone with God is essential to the power behind our influence in this life. We can't be scared anymore. We can't fear getting close to God because we don't want to feel bad about who we are. It's not that we're bad people. God doesn't see us that way. That's how this world and the people in it view it.

God sees someone created for a purpose. He sees things as they will be (Romans 4:17). As you will be. He looks at you with eyes of grace and with fullness of mercy. Beyond the limits of space and time. You are a vessel to flow truth and reflect His light. A bold candle that cannot be easily blown out.

The Lord has a plan to cultivate revival within you.

The power of God is beyond our comprehension. We are humans with carnal minds. Our abilities are nothing compared to the Omnipotent One. Yet for some reason the Lord gave us the gift of making our own choices. The Great Creator, Master of the Universe, The Holy One allows us to freely choose right or wrong. To choose His way or our own. Why would He do that? I don't think you or I would have created this system and yet here we are. We are daily given that power. *It is within this powerful gift that we are challenged.* How will our choices play out daily? How will our small choices make a big difference, not only in our lives but those we're connected to? How will one choice we make affect the choice of someone else? The decision can be a good or bad influence for us or the next generation. The results become the blocks in which our children will be guided on.

Your power to choose comes from the heart of a loving and merciful God.

Making choices isn't glamorous. Oftentimes, we have to make choices alone without any fanfare or applause. And it's easy to be full of anxiety about it. Just thinking about the choices we have to make is hard enough. Then throw in *how* it will affect those around us. *Phew!* The weight can be unbearable, but I think that's why God gave us the power to choose. *If there was no pressure, would we run to Him?* That sounds awful but let's think about it a moment. He lets us freely make choices every day. In that freedom, we can choose to serve Him or not. *Isn't there more power in service that is genuine than forced - to serve because we want to?*

Sadly, it doesn't cross our minds very often. I never used to think about it. When we don't quietly connect with our Lord, we lose that spiritual filter. Our mouths are loose with overly salty words. Our boastful attitudes pollute the atmosphere in every space we walk into. Our pent-up unforgiveness is a sword against reconciliation. Our hearts are hardened towards the unsaved and we often treat them as if they are unlovable. *And God weeps.*

Picture a lake at your feet. Your toes are buried between the warm sand and the cool water. A smooth stone dances between your fingertips. You wind up and release. As the stone hits the fragile surface of the water, waves from the impact ripple outward and the still water is now a wavy mirror, reflecting the impact of your decision. Now, I want you to picture someone you love standing silently in the lake. Bubbles splashing on their shoulders and water droplets on their chin. They have been touched by your choice in some way. Your focus may not have been on them - perhaps your gaze was upon the stone itself - but wherever your eyes were, the reality is clear: choices are powerful.

Your influence is real.

Recently I told my six-year-old son David "I don't want you to make waves". It came naturally even though it's not a phrase I've ever used. David is very inquisitive and detailed oriented. He didn't miss a beat, questioning what I just said to him. It took me a moment to think as his big brown eyes waited for an answer. I knew painting him a verbal illustration would help him understand.

"Water is still. It's quiet and peaceful. Until a boat comes by and the calm water turns into waves. There might be a situation that we're in and we might not like it. If we respond in a calm way, we don't make waves. If we respond like the boat, loud and fast, we make waves and it can be uncomfortable for the people around us. God wants us to respond in a peaceful way. Not in a way that will make it more difficult for other people or ourselves."

I usually know when he has gotten the point of one of our chats when he sits still and his eyes are focused. His brain is pondering, mulling over the information. It's cute to watch him! But I always want to make sure he understands what I say, so I asked him if it made sense. He slowly nodded and that was the end of the conversation. It clicked, he processed it and only time will tell if he will apply it. This doesn't always happen when I speak to him but how rewarding it feels when it does! I thank the Lord often for helping me simplify big topics so that the mind of my child can get the principles.

I don't want my son to be a doormat and never speak up but there's a difference when God is involved and when we've chosen not to involve Him. *Our words and actions can't be undone or taken back.* We can't plead hard enough with God to reverse them. Negotiations are not part of the system. The ripples have already started and people have already been touched. Your words and your actions are now out into the atmosphere. The question is: *how will your choices influence the lives of those that surround you?*

Influence is the capacity to have an effect on the character, development or behavior of someone, or something or the effect itself.

Being creative is therapeutic for me. So when the word "glitter" kept coming to my mind during my studio and prayer times, I didn't think much about it. Then Gods started impressing upon me this message. At first, I didn't quite understand the concept the Lord was so graciously sharing. The more He unveiled, the more I broke. I knew He was speaking to the sin within me. *That I was neglecting to use the power of influence to glorify Him in all the areas of my life.* In the way I spoke to my husband, how I talked to my children and the emotions I was allowing myself to camp in. My heart is in these pages. Not to boast of myself but to inspire you to turn your eyes to Jesus! To bring forth a message that we all need in this fast-paced, conceited world.

Choices affect everyone and sin is never exclusive.

Have you ever spilled glitter? Glitter is very difficult to get back into the bottle once it gets out. You may be able to scoop most of it up but not all of it. It gets everywhere and is careless about what it touches. Glitter is savage! It's attractive but a hot mess at the same time. There's something so powerful about it. The way it looks like a billion mini mirrors of pure light. *Our influence is like glitter.*

When an influential glitter bomb has exploded, those around us are covered in the aftermath. If the influence has a negative tone, we can probably gain forgiveness about our reactive behavior or choice *after* it has been released. The truth is when it's done, it's done. This is when we must realize the need for our Savior and the need to make intentional choices that will bring positive tones to our influence, before we hurt the ones we love. In those vulnerable moments when we see how we've hurt someone, we should always talk to Jesus first. *We must get closer to God!* Just by existing on this earth, we have influence. Each one of us, whether we want to or not. This influence is essential to our human relationships and our testimony as Christians.

"Understanding is a wellspring of life unto him that hath it: but the instruction of fools is folly. The heart of the wise teacheth his mouth, and addeth learning to his lips. Pleasant words are as an honeycomb, sweet to the soul, and health to the bones." (Proverbs 16:22-24)

The minute I believe the lie that sin is only my problem, is the moment I've placed my influence into the hands of the enemy. I can't believe that lie. You can't believe that lie. *Sin can never be my personal problem without impacting other people.* If we give into the lie that sin is exclusively ours, even without realizing it, we have given Satan the influence over our legacy. Sin doesn't care who our parents are. Sin doesn't care about our church status, family dynamics or career position. All it needs is a vessel to travel through. *Sin will never stop at influencing only one person.* We can break the cycle with the help of the Healer. I'm starting to realize that wallowing in guilt only keeps me focused on the sin and not the Savior. This taints the influence I have and other people around me won't benefit from it. But if I can get my eyes on my Redeemer, change can take place. Chains can be broken and the lives that touch mine will be affected in the most beautiful, holiest of ways.

Sin will keep jumping from person to person until someone says, "No, not anymore. That stops here. It stops with me. Right now, in Jesus' name!"

In the book of Genesis, with the help of the subtle serpent, Eve thought God was keeping good things from her and made a terrible choice. Although Adam was the authority over her, allowing her to be deceived and manipulate him, it was Eve's decision to sin. It didn't only affect her. *It changed the course of history.* To this day, women are still reaping the fruit of Eve's behavior (Genesis 3:16). Let that sink into our minds a bit. One choice made thousands of years ago altered life for people not even born yet! How would Eve feel today, looking around and seeing the changes her sin has brought to society? How broken would the "mother of all living" be?

She couldn't have imagined her choice mattering so much but it did. *And our choices matter too.*

Eve felt the tragic loss of a child when one son murdered the other. A heavy heart was not something the Lord wanted for the special woman made of man's rib. As a mother of two boys myself, I can't even imagine that sort of pain. I truly believe the story of Cain and Abel carries many messages for us today, including how the influence of one can affect the lives of many. How one choice changed the course for one family, kicking them out of paradise and causing their children to wrestle with their own choices.

Sin is a time traveler and we need to say "time is up!"

When fear is involved, Satan is not too far. Fear takes victims and will never let them go. The only way that fear will flee is when the victim turns their eyes upon the Victor! It is then that Satan *must* flee (James 4:7). He is not given any other options. God doesn't give the enemy choices when it comes to the power of His Identity. The moment we follow the Deliverer, instead of fear, we step over the line to the winning side, the place where love abides. This is how the cycle of sin is broken. If we hold onto fear, we get fed false truths and start to have backwards thinking. *How far will our influence go if we stop allowing fear to make choices for us?*

The Glitter Effect is our influence and the choices we make.

It is the imprint we leave with those around us and how it can spread. *It is our legacy.* Our choices can be either nourishing or damaging. The root of this influence depends on our foundation with God and the daily walk.

It is incredibly important, taking that quiet time with Him seriously. Asking the Lord questions and waiting for the answers without jumping to conclusions or assumptions. Without the right structure of support, it doesn't matter how far we go spiritually. If we even go far at all. The connection between creation and Creator must be alive and active.

When God is at the center, our influence can help create a masterpiece. We can reflect the Light. *A tiny speck of influence can be the difference between a positive or negative message.* When our choices are in line with His will, there is hope for the daily influence we have right now and the legacy we leave behind. When we stand on Christ, the Solid Rock, He becomes our Anchor and strength. He becomes the Captain of our emotional ships, leading us away from the dangerous storms and safely toward the shore. When God is at the center, our influence can reflect Him! To shimmer for His glory.

There's a hymn that goes:

Turn your eyes upon Jesus,

Look full in His wonderful face,

And the things of earth will grow strangely dim,

In the light of His glory and grace.

It is time to turn our eyes and look up! To look to Jesus, truly see Him for who He is and not for who we *want* Him to be. To experience the light of His glory and grace. That light will change our vision. Things become clearer. Real life, hashtag no filter because Jesus *is* the filter. When His light cuts through the fog, our sight is enlightened. The things of this world don't seem so important anymore. He has bigger and better plans for us. Once we connect with the lover of our souls and He changes us, our influence has more potential to leave a positive impact.

Our choices never affect only ourselves.

If we understood this concept, imagine the heartaches that would never happen. Many of us are allowing fear to drive away God's light. Fear of rejection. Fear of commitment. Fear of the unknown. *Fear of not being in control.* Maybe we've formed bad habits and aren't taking time with Him like we should. Or maybe we're scared because we can't see the entire picture of what God is doing. We find it hard to trust Him. In this internal battle, we become self-focused instead of Christ-focused. While the Lord's light continually is shining, we are blinded by our own personal emotions. This must change in order for us to be the change this world needs. For Jesus to be glorified and revival to happen in the hearts of His people.

God is still working on me. You'll probably see that if we spend more than 30 minutes together. Which is why this message is real to me. It's something God revealed so I can learn and grow. As a person, wife and mother. He continues to open my eyes to the influence I have. And while it's super scary and I wish I didn't have such influence, it's also empowering because God has chosen us to be His people. *He has a purpose for me and for you!* The Lord has a special place carved out that only you can fill. He's not trying to be a tyrant, controlling our every move. Our Father is loving and wants us to be examples of His love to others. How awesome is our God! The life of a Christian is longsuffering but not without help. God has promised to always be there if we need Him, but we must do better. *I must do better.* I don't want to just reach to God when I'm drowning. I want to be by His side so consistently that as the danger approaches, I can hear the sweet voice of my Shepherd so I don't sink. Through obedience to God, others can have an opportunity to stay above water as well.

I'd be a fool to think I could say or do whatever I wanted without repercussions.

And yet, that's *exactly* what this world keeps telling us, especially as women. To speak from "your heart" or what's on "your mind" without fear of consequences. While it is okay to voice your opinion, there is a time and a place. There is also a tone and a language that can hinder the message. Or worse, distort it. There are also some things that should remain inside while our mouths stay shut. Navigating our emotions is a battle and the Lord should be our General, giving us the orders to move forward or stand down.

"The heart is deceitful above all things, and desperately wicked: who can know it? I the Lord search the heart, I try the reins, even to give every man according to his ways, and according to the fruit of his doings."
(Jeremiah 17:9-10)

Yes, I will fail again. Yes, I will have bad days. And yes (thank you, Jesus) I have been blessed with resources, so I can surround myself with life-giving influences, to turn it all around! I don't have to camp out in my feelings and obsess about the situation. I don't have to stay where I am. I can be moved and changed. I can shift to align myself with my Creator. *And you can too!* That's a blessing right there. To have the choice to choose God's way. To choose the better way. That's powerful. I don't think we honor it enough. That the God of Heaven would make Himself available for our benefit. He didn't have to. The Lord didn't have to become the spotless Lamb, but He did. Once and for all! (2 Corinthians 5:15) To slay sin in the grave and shake the gates of Hell to its core. *What have we to fear if God is on our side?*

If He has fought for us to be free, then let's choose freedom.

If God has given us the power to choose being a light to shine forth, then we need to shine for Him! *We owe Him that and so much more.* When I see my influence is starting to be toxic, I try to replenish it. On those hard days, where I feel my influence hasn't been as positive as it should have been, I first talk to God through prayer and reading the Word. I do this daily, but I make my prayers specific to the issue at hand and I'm more intentional with the scriptures I read. It will cut through the darkness and reveal the truth. I also follow uplifting accounts on social media. I pull out my favorite conference CDs featuring powerful, Apostolic teaching. I've also streamed recorded worship services on our television. I reach out to those friends who are anointed during conversations, that can speak life-giving words that I need to hear.

"And he shall be like a tree planted by the rivers of water, that bringeth forth his fruit in his season; his leaf also shall not wither; and whatsoever he doeth shall prosper." (Psalm 1:3)

Influence works two ways: it goes out and it comes in. It's like the very air we breathe. Trees needs oxygen to thrive. If we are told to "be like a tree", but have we tapped into a pure oxygen source? Or are we trying to recirculate tainted air quality, expecting a different result?

We are called to be separate, not just in word or deed, but also what we take in (2 Corinthians 6:17). Every day we are gathering data. Emotions and mindsets are being deposited. We must be discerning about what influences us, so we can be better equipped when our influence goes out into the world.

Why should we be planted like a tree by the rivers of water? That's how we can survive. Pull from the soil the nutrients provided by the life-giving water source. We will always have influence. That won't change. What will change is our awareness of it and how to use it. We cannot change people, but we can change how we react. When we are living according to His truth, it brings opportunity for change to happen in the lives of others.

Our values must be in the fabric of who we are.

Truth will always separate the darkness from the light. That means not everyone needs to be comfortable with the truth God gives you. We can't worry about what people think when we're living for God. *We need to care more about what God thinks of us.* If we look at truth as an option, we'll probably never choose it. Truth has to be a non-negotiable factor in how we live our lives. Part of that is being honest with ourselves. Sometimes the truth hurts. Sometimes it requires change. *If we are to share the gospel, we must be truthful, so we can then be trustworthy.* I don't think God gave us the power of influence to watch others fall. We are called to rise higher than where we are and go farther than where we're planning on going. During this process, with the right influence, we can also bring others higher.

"But ye are a chosen generation, a royal priesthood, an holy nation, a peculiar people; that ye should shew forth

the praises of him who hath called you out of darkness into his marvellous light"
(1 Peter 2:9)

The purpose of glitter was always to improve aesthetic or decorate a surface. In ancient times it was created by using glass, crushing certain insects like beetles or by scraping shiny minerals and rocks, such as mica and malachite. It was then applied to cave paintings or used as a cosmetic dust for people's faces. In 1934, a New Jersey farmer and machinist named Henry Ruschmann discovered a way to make glitter by using scrap plastics. He went on to be the founder of Meadowbrook Inventions, a company that continues to make industrial glitter today.

There are different things that contribute to our influence but the purpose must always stay the same. We must use it to glorify the King and bring edification to those around us (1 Thessalonians 5:11). *The purpose of glitter never changed, only how it was used.* It was beautiful and was applied to enhance whatever it touched. The Lord has designed influence to enhance our testimony which brings forth His truth and advances His kingdom. Our influence will affect anything or anyone it touches. Glitter sticks wherever it lands and our influence does the same.

"Jesus saith unto him, I am the way, the truth, and the life: no man cometh unto the Father, but by me."
(John 14:6)

We want so bad to push back the gates of hell for the Kingdom but many times we don't properly consult the only One who can do it! We take matters into our own hands, take steps into our own plans, and wonder why there isn't a miracle. *We leave the Miracle Worker behind, then claim it wasn't His will because the results were not to our liking.* But what if we paused before reaching, prayed before speaking and read the Bible before walking?

We can't be His hands and feet without His heart and mind.

We get so focused on the tools to do work, but we don't make more of an effort to prepare ourselves inwardly. Being His hands and feet are great but we need the proper intentions, motives and spiritual disciplines. Being His hands and feet isn't the entire equation. It's the result of having His heart and mind. *The only way people can do great things for God is listening to what He thinks and what He feels.* Knowing His character and His desires. Jesus is the way, the truth and the life. He is the One who can show us the way, open our eyes to the truth and give life through the influence He has blessed us with.

We were born in this time for a reason.

This is the Glitter Effect. Knowing who God is so our influence can shine for Him in a world that is growing darker every day. We don't have to be afraid that our influence won't make a difference. It will. *If you plant yourself by the Living Water and drink up everything He has to give you.* Grow strong in faith, resilient in the pursuit of truth and branch out to give good fruit so others can be fed. This should be our heart's desire.

This prayer should realign our attention. We don't have perfect words but we can connect to the One who created words. He'll take care of the content. We are responsible for the delivery.

Lord, what freedom we've been given to choose Your way! It is because of Your love that we have the power of choice. Thank you for giving us the chance to change. To be better people and to be better influences. Let us not be fearful of this world or any opposition. For greater are You within us than any powers in this world! Help us overcome self-doubt, shame and anxiety. In this victory, You can be glorified as we shine Your goodness. Let our testimonies be rooted in truth. Give us the proper boldness to do and say what is right. So we may become more like You and influence those around us to seek You for themselves. In Jesus' name, Amen.

2

Shrapnel

"If you are defeated, it's because you've already accepted defeat. Remember that the negative voices are not in control of your destiny. Jesus is."

Rev. Brian Kinsey

Words have power. God created the world and everything in it with His words (Genesis 1 and John 1). With this in mind, it shouldn't be a surprise to us when we listen to negative words the results will also be negative. The same is true for our actions. Negative seeds can sprout negative actions. *It's one of my greatest beliefs that the war against believers today and future generations are the negative voices we allow to become our internal compass.* Those voices transform our identity to something God never intended. They become the voice we use to speak to other people. They are given more attention and the soft voice of our Shepherd is silenced.

"For they that are after the flesh do mind the things of the flesh; but they that are after the Spirit the things of the Spirit. For to be carnally minded is death; but to be spiritually minded is life and peace."
(Romans 8:5-6)

Henry Shrapnel was an English soldier and inventor, born in the summer of 1761. At 18 years old, he began his military career. It wasn't long before his scientific talents were utilized to better the artillery. Henry kept the details of his project private and over the course of many long years, he was finally ready to introduce the fruit of his labor. Henry had designed a shell that once fired, a timer would make it explode, releasing small lead contents into the air. It would cause serious harm to any enemy soldiers within its path. Henry's invention was very effective and by 1799 he was able to see it in action. He continued working successfully, earning many ranks within the military. His vision and passion for his work changed the history of battle. Henry never would've imagined how much influence he had and just how powerful his influence was for future generations.

We hear the term "*shrapnel*" used when describing pieces of an object that have broken with excessive force upon an explosion. They are fragments of a once solid material. There are countless war stories about soldiers being wounded because they were struck by shrapnel. So much force was initiated in the beginning that when the object broke apart, what was left had enough power to be just as dangerous a bullet.

Our words and actions can be like shrapnel.

Influence is important yet we spend little time slowing down to say and do the right thing. I think we know we must get better, but we don't take the time to understand how our choices become other people's experiences. The Glitter Effect is a two-way street. Our negativity affects those around us. We don't live on an island all by ourselves, as much as we would probably love that! God created us to be among each other. We have the choice to give more love if we choose to. It requires submission and discipline. *So often we are either numb or bored in our pursuit of internal purity.* We have formed bad social habits and have become blind to those habits. Our conversations are often one sided, putting ourselves at the center instead of being good listeners.

Others around us are being emotionally affected by the shrapnel of our choices.

"For he that will love life, and see good days, let him refrain his tongue from evil, and his lips that they speak no guile: Let him eschew evil, and do good; let him seek peace, and ensue it.
(1 Peter 3:10-11)

As a mom, it's the hardest thing to filter my internal attitude so it doesn't become my outer voice. I find myself being quick to brag about being full of His Spirit and yet my words are filthy. It doesn't have to be the actual language that's negative. It can be my tone, motive, the way it's expressed. The same goes for how we speak to our spouses or our friends. There's no room for "mean girls" in God's Kingdom. There should be no room for negative speaking within us.

"Pleasant words are as an honeycomb, sweet to the soul, and health to the bones."
(Proverbs 16:24)

The Lord will not stop us from speaking love to someone else. That is the root of who He is (1 John 4:8). If love is not represented, it's on us. We need to start being accountable or the future generation will suffer. I don't want my boys to remember about my reactive behaviors when reminiscing about their childhood memories. I don't want my husband to have the impression that his wife can't control an outburst or an unkind accusation without approaching the situation with maturity. I also don't want to impose upon friends or family members with emotions that I should have kept to myself but didn't, emotions that were not filtered but rather lashed out with powerful passion. I'm not saying we can't have opinions or feelings but when we acknowledge those things, we need to be careful *how* we share them with the world, and really, if we truly need to share them at all!

Desperately chase God not just for His blessings but for your transformation.

Being reactive might feel good at first but it only lasts a minute before we feel the weight of what was said or done. It isn't worth it when we look at the bigger picture. *The eternal picture.* Are we helping people get to Heaven or hindering their journey? Our influence can make significant imprints in the hearts of others. It is our responsibility to make sure the Lord Jesus Christ is the filter of our words and actions. He is a gentleman and will let us make the choice without force. It's my personal prayer that over time, it will become second nature for me to spiritually check myself in certain social situations. I do see a change, but I know He's not done with me yet. God can work through a donkey and He can work through stubborn kings. This brings me hope that he can work through a strong-willed, selfish person like me.

"A good man out of the good treasure of his heart bringeth forth that which is good; and an evil man out of the evil treasure of his heart bringeth forth that which is evil: for of the abundance of the heart his mouth speaketh."
(Luke 6:45)

I already shared how glitter can be a hot mess. I'm sure you already had some experience with glitter before reading this book, so can you agree that it goes everywhere. Glitter can cause chaos and create an atmosphere of panic. At the same time, glitter is beautiful, like shiny stars in your hands. Glitter paper, glitter glue, glitter clothes, glitter paint, *I want it all.* If I treat glitter with respect and I'm intentional about how I use it, then I can construct a work of art. The same applies to the influence we have. We must be responsible before our influence gets transmitted into the air and into the lives of others. If any shrapnel should fly, let it be His love through our brokenness.

"The sacrifices of God are a broken spirit: a broken and a contrite heart, O God, thou wilt not despise."
(Psalm 51:17)

    I want everything I say and everything I do to be rooted in love. *I want people to see Him through me.* When they hear something that I have said, I hope it will be a reflection of His goodness. I want to be better, not bitter. Quick to forgive, and not cause division. To have harmony and truth in the threads of my conversations and behavior. The bigger picture points to Jesus. I want my Glitter Effect to help save souls. To ripple across my days filled with His Spirit and creating a legacy of holiness.

Be an example in private, not only in public.

    Behind closed doors, our most intimate thoughts and the words we tell our heart should be pure in motive and contrite in spirit. *True integrity is being the same alone as we are around people.* There have been many times where I've asked God to use me. I would be discouraged because He seemed silent. Until I opened my spiritual eyes and realized He hadn't been silent at all. I was just listening to the wrong voices. I was unwilling to listen to God's full commandment. *A soldier is not obedient if they obey half the instruction.* It's still disobedience. You see, what happens when no one is around is a sacred opportunity to still worship the One we praise in public. We should lift up our hands in our own home by ourselves and not only in a church service. Our prayer life *should* be part of our life and not just a cute phrase we say. We are His soldiers and have a job to do but we're too busy to hear everything He is trying to say.

We desire change in others more than in ourselves.

It has to start with us. We have to start pursuing Jesus more than the way we are pursuing everything else. Private devotion is essential to survival as a soldier of the Lord. A heartfelt prayer life is essential to how we thrive as an army. *I have to make sure to seek God first to create a movement within myself before I try to move in this world.* I can't be afraid to listen to the entire instruction God has for me. I can't be focused on only the safe parts. There's a quote I came across that helps put things into perspective.

"A ship is always safe at shore but that is not what it's built for."

Albert Einstein

How will we use this power of influence? Will we abuse it and be irresponsible? Reactive instead of proactive? Or will we be intentional and purposeful so that our choices glorify the One who has changed us? The decision is made right now. *Today.* We have to choose to be the light and not create shadows in the lives of those around us. By His grace and mercy, we have this opportunity. To shimmer for His Kingdom. To shine for His purpose.

"Create in me a clean heart, O God, and renew a right spirit within me."

(Psalm 51:10)

Prevention. It is the act of stopping something from happening, preventing an action that may cause hindrance, whether to yourself or others around you. It's a lost art in a society that has made glorifying self-gratification a normal thing. We have normalized personal attacks against one another to fulfill our internal desire of being heard, so we can be right, even if we are wrong. They've been hit by our verbal darts and we couldn't care less. *Shrapnel.* How do we prevent shooting out verbal bullets? How do we prevent being selfish? How can we prevent hurting the ones we love?

"Hurt people, hurt people."

Will Bowen

Nothing can be truer! Explosions need a fuse. If we've been alive long enough, we might have years of heartbreak, deception and mistrust. That's a lot of sparks for the fire. I can see it with myself. This entire process of studying and writing needed to happen first before God showed me the fuses, fuses that I still held in my hands every day. Story after story of verbal and emotional shrapnel that had wounded me. And I was still holding them all. Days, weeks, months, years later, *I thought I was healed but I was deflecting the way the Lord wanted to heal me.* Explosives that remained hidden deep within myself, waiting for a fuse.

He wants to relieve harmful pressure to make us new.

Instead of burying them under the blood, they became the power behind releasing more shrapnel into the atmosphere around me. I was pulling the trigger when God wanted me to hand over the weapon. God doesn't want us pretending we're okay. He desires for us to be fully healed and live honestly in that testimony. When we allow the Lord to fully take over, that's when we no longer are affected by fuses because the explosive no longer exists! This will save other lives besides our own.

"If any man among you seem to be religious, and bridleth not his tongue, but deceiveth his own heart, this man's religion is vain."
(James 1:26)

I was at a conference earlier this year when something happened that caught me by surprise. Have you ever been in a situation where it made you so uncomfortable, you didn't even know what to do? I didn't expect it which is why I didn't say what I should have. I overheard a girl speaking to her group of friends. They were watching people exit the sanctuary of the church. The service had ended, and everyone was gathering around the vendor tables and mingling in the hall. The tone of this girl's voice cut through the calm. It was drenched in judgment and distaste. She whispered to her friends about another girl's appearance and made the comment that her sister was more beautiful. In just a few words, she polluted the air with toxic negativity and involved other people in her opinion about someone else. I heard her but didn't speak up. I guess I was in shock because we just had an amazing move of God during church. The Holy Ghost was alive and working. That moment she made comments about a stranger, it caused the rest of the group to zone in on the target. I don't know whether they joined the ambush of verbal abuse or not. I walked away and now I wish I would have spoken some correction. I don't share this to gossip but to give an example. My heart hurts for her because she missed out on a blessing. Even if she was touched during the service, the miracle she could be waiting for might be delayed because of the way her heart spoke that night.

"Surely he hath borne our griefs, and carried our sorrows: yet we did esteem him stricken, smitten of God, and afflicted.

But he was wounded for our transgressions, he was bruised for our iniquities: the chastisement of our peace was upon him; and with his stripes we are healed."
(Isaiah 53:4-5)

God is not omnipresent wherever *we* choose Him to be. He *is* everywhere, all the time! We can't control what He hears because He hears it all. It's scary to think we've become numb to His presence once we walk out the double doors of the sanctuary. It's almost like we leave our Christian selves in the pew and put back on the carnal persona on our way out. Are we waiting for a miracle in which God sends an angel to save us from the pain we have inside? *That's what the cross was for!* I feel like we do expect God to do more than Calvary. We want signs and wonders other than Him dying for sin. We've been given the Word and prayer for open communication. *Is that not enough to change us?*

He has called us to be the light, not lightning.

It's not our place to zap other people to the point of burning their confidence. We can gently guide or even boldly correct, but with the right ammo, and with the right heart. Having pure motives doesn't mean they are perfect motives. Only God is perfect. Motives should be sincere, without malice. If we keep spreading fire, then we're going to burn down from the inside, out. We must elevate our conversations especially with other daughters of the King. We're called to be royalty so it's time to start acting like it. We are princesses and heirs to the inheritance. We should be poised with purpose, and intentional about our voices and the messages we are leaving behind.

Stop striving for perfection and start aiming for purity.

God alone has the power to change our hearts with holy cleanliness. This change will mold the motives behind our words and actions. *When we try to fix ourselves, we are doing everyone a disservice.* We can't take on that much work! How can one human heart fix another human heart? How can creation play the role of Creator? We would leave ourselves still hurting from past wounds. There would still be war taking place within us.

"When thou saidst, Seek ye my face; my heart said unto thee, Thy face, Lord, will I seek."
(Psalm 27:8)

When we seek His face instead of seeking our own way to fix things, our way of thinking is transformed. I think we stare at ourselves too much in the mirror, dissecting every flaw and blemish. We feel unworthy but God is telling each of us to turn our gaze fully onto Him. We are given a new look at what reality is through the eyes of the Lord Jesus. We were bought with a price no one can repay or replace!

Soldiers prevent injury by following a plan and watching each other's backs.

They don't deviate. They don't act spontaneous when lives are on the line. It is not fun and games on the battlefield. One wrong move could be fatal. They are geared up and equipped with the right tools. They have what they need to achieve victory. *We need to treat our sin this same way.* We have become entertained by sin that we often joke about it. Sometimes we laugh it off and we might even say "I'm working on it" with a half-smile.

God has a plan for us, so what I'm about to say next isn't new. You've probably heard it since Sunday School or preached over the pulpit your entire life. Maybe you've been in the church so long, it all sounds boring. I get it. There is a reason why those in leadership positions keep teaching about this over and over. *Casualties.* Every year, souls fall away. People walk out and never return. The battle was going on, but they were an island of one. Their hearts sailed away without the Anchor. Not because He wasn't available. *His directions weren't applied.*

"For the word of God is quick, and powerful, and sharper than any two-edged sword, piercing even to the dividing asunder of soul and spirit, and of the joints and marrow, and is a discerner of the thoughts and intents of the heart."
(Hebrews 4:12)

I'm talking about getting into the Word of God. Reading and studying it for ourselves. *Prayer.* Kneeling in humble adoration for a Creator who spoke and the universe appeared. *What more can He do to show us that He is able?* Trust. Obey. Worship who He has showed Himself to be. Not who we want Him to be. The Lord Jesus Christ, after forming all that we know and see, became a man. The Almighty humbled Himself and walked among the very trees He made. He felt every single emotion we feel. He listened to weeping faces, held the babies of the Gentiles, and ate with the greatest sinners in history. *All for love.*

He was then led to a hill that He had created. The perfect Lamb was sacrificed for our sin, everyone's sin, and three days later, a grave was missing a body. There was life again! He was received up in glory and sent His Spirit down, so that He not only created us and dwelt among us but now through the Holy Ghost, God could be in us! *What else can He do for us that has not already been done?*

We don't need more evidence. We need repentance.

We sit and complain. We whine and mumble. We speak false accusations, criticize our pastors, scowl at non-church people and call ourselves "Christians". The Greatest Soldier laid down His life for us so that we may lay down our lives for others. It may not be in the physical. I believe God is calling us to lay down our pride so He can work in us to bring to pass what has been in His plan from the beginning.

"Every word of God is pure: he is a shield unto them that put their trust in him."
(Proverbs 30:5)

There is no magic pill or special password. We must unify our hearts with the heart of the Lord Jesus Christ. Put on the full armor, not just the pieces that are convenient for the moment. If we want to be a helpful soldier, then we need to gear up. Obey the Word. Listen to authority. Pray for those who hurt us and pray for those who don't. Have compassion for the ones who have never set foot in a church. Have compassion for those who have but it's been a long time. *Be light.* Shine mercy and grace the way God has shined it on all of us. Guard your tongue, swallow nasty words and repent. Unroll your eyes and repent again. Hide scripture in your mind so that it is a sharp weapon when needed. Prepare before the day starts. Be thankful at the end of it. *Be intentional.* Preparation, prevention, purity. Soldiers before us left breadcrumbs already. You don't have to reinvent the wheel. Just let Jesus drive!

We can be a vessel used for a bigger purpose.

When we are influenced by His Word and by His power, it is then that pure influence is birthed into our stories. There is, of course, another side to this truth. If we neglect our personal time with the Lord, it's not only our souls at stake. Our influence suffers and the voice we have been given is muffled by our disobedience. Ignoring the problems won't make them go away. We'll have to face them again. David understood this breach. His choices created shrapnel that reached many lives beyond his own. Eventually repentance had its way in his heart. He spent time with God, healing and learning. *He is an example of someone who saw his mistakes and wanted a different ending.* David remembered the God of his youth. The songs he sang while watching the sheep. He desired to go back to where God first met him. In Psalm 62:1-3, David says:

"Truly my soul waiteth upon God: from him cometh my salvation. He only is my rock and my salvation; he is my defence; I shall not be greatly moved. How long will ye imagine mischief against a man? ye shall be slain all of you: as a bowing wall shall ye be, and as a tottering fence."

We are told to be still and wait. We are told to trust in the Lord. We are told to have faith, to not fear and He will take care of us. The scripture is full of this promise. Yet we continue to embrace our sin like it's a treasure. Our fists are so clenched around it that our knuckles are turning white. Our focus is off the One who created us with purpose. We are choosing to make choices for the here and now, rather than for eternity. Sometimes we are too close to something to see the chains. It's when we step back, we can see the bigger picture. I've learned that if God tells me no, it's enough. My Father knows what will help or hinder me. He deals in eternity and I need to trust in His plans. This world is not my home. Heaven is the destination. That might mean I have to listen to God when no one else understands why.

Our influence has been breached and we are unaware.

A breach is a gap or a broken wall. It doesn't have to be big. A small crack branches out to a larger issue. A wall cannot stand if it's not strong. The sins we are worshiping in our lives are leaving us weak in the spirit (1 John 2:15). We are like a wall that is about to crumble. One gust of wind can send us away from the hands of the Creator. While our Shepherd is patiently waiting for His sheep to turn to Him for rest and comfort, we are foolishly chasing earthly things. We are allowing our eyes to lose focus. It is weakening the testimony of our influence.

"Wherefore thus saith the Holy One of Israel, Because ye despise this word, and trust in oppression and perverseness, and stay thereon: Therefore this iniquity shall be to you as a breach ready to fall, swelling out in a high wall, whose breaking cometh suddenly at an instant."
(Isaiah 30:12-13)

Sin isn't a point in history. It's not a pin on a map. *It takes captive life breathing creations made for a Godly purpose and perverts their understanding.* It takes a legacy meant for good and destroys the path, leading to a destructive future. It keeps saint's prisoner, focusing their hearts on selfish desires and the lust of the flesh.

Sin lies by saying no one will hurt if we disobey God.

That's a word straight from the pit! Sin is never about just one person. It doesn't affect one soul. *It is contagious and will influence the lives around us.* A sin committed in private never remains private. Whatever we do in the dark will come into the light and be exposed, all the while cracking our foundations until our walls become so weak, we can no longer stand, and then we break.

"For nothing is secret, that shall not be made manifest; neither any thing hid, that shall not be known and come abroad."
(Luke 8:17)

On the outside, it will seem like a quick lifestyle change. It will come as a surprise to loved ones and the church, sending confusion into the minds of those who care. We call it "backsliding" but it's really an internal breakage. For those who have never received or seen the redemptive power of God, this breakage seems like the end. They feel like they have no hope. In war, a soldier has compassion towards another soldier who has suffered a wound. A soldier following the right orders wouldn't rush over to drive more pain into them, kicking them lower when their faces are already kissing the dirt. *That's something a traitor would do.*

Be cautious when someone delights in others suffering.

People are people. We will go through hard times, it's a fact. We might not handle situations the way we should because we are in much turmoil. As fellow soldiers in Christ, we need to do better. Encourage the healing. Usher them back to an altar. Prop up their arms if they become weary. Our knees should always bend first in prayer. We should never use our power of influence to damage another brother or sister on purpose. The enemy delights in that because we are doing his dirty work for him. *Instead, a soldier should comfort them to help them survive.* We don't have to have all the answers. We're not called to have them all! We are only commanded to love God and love people just like God does.

"Beware of false prophets, which come to you in sheep's clothing, but inwardly they are ravening wolves."
(Matthew 7:15)

What do we do if we see someone wounded by spiritual shrapnel? What is our place as a fellow soldier in Christ when another soldier is slowing down, about to collapse? Encourage them to make it right with God. Give them scripture that will build them up again. *Listen to them.* Be there for them. They don't need any more inflicted pain. We must give them hope. We must give them Jesus!

"And he shall break it as the breaking of the potters' vessel that is broken in pieces; he shall not spare: so that there shall not be found in the bursting of it a sherd to take fire from the hearth, or to take water withal out of the pit."
(Isaiah 30:14)

The breach could break us down so much, we will be useless in the hands of the Potter and can't be used for the purpose He intended us for. Not only will our sin destroy us inside but it will destroy the positive power of our influence. We will never be without influence. Either we will be in line with His will and our influence will bring prosperity to His Kingdom, or it will be used to push people away from the Lord and deeper into sin. It starts with our one-on-one time with God and the influence of His Word in us.

Our choices will drive the way our influence is used.

God is full of mercy and has offered a solution. We have no excuses. He gives us hope when we are hopeless and grace when we feel worthless. The Lord patiently waits for us to commit to Him. When we finally turn to Him, we are given what we need to be free from the chains of sin and the healing of the breach can begin.

"For thus saith the Lord GOD, the Holy One of Israel; In returning and rest shall ye be saved; in quietness and in confidence shall be your strength: and ye would not." (Isaiah 30:15)

Stubbornness is death. Instead of choosing to be silent and still in the Lord, to allow Him to repair the breach, some people continue in their sins. They follow appealing flickering lights, while inside they are breaking. He wants us to return to rest in Him. To be confident in Him and to be still in the quietness of His mercy as the repairs are made. As the Lord heals the hurting in time, our heart is made whole. In time, we can be used for His intended purpose. The scripture says that *"ye would not"* or *"you would not,"* meaning that even though there is a choice to be redeemed, the person receiving instruction didn't choose God's way. So as we walk as soldiers with new eyes, let us ask these two questions to make sure we're in line with our General:

Will you not allow Him to heal the breach through quiet communion with Him?

Will you release positive influence as a soldier of God?

3

Foundations

"He's not looking for the perfect. He's looking for the available."

Natalie Grant

For years my husband Jonathan and I prayed for a house. Living in a condo was putting a strain on our family. We wanted a place where we could grow. As time went by, we felt the Lord impress upon us that it was the right time to finally purchase our first house. We scheduled appointments to view homes in town but none of them were right for us. At the end of our search, there were two houses left and we met with our realtor at the first one. It was a cute little white house with amazing features. Between the two houses, this was the one I was the most excited to see.

This could be it! I had thought.

Oh. It was definitely *not* it. Long cracks scaled the ceiling in the main living areas. When we got down to the basement, we noticed a very big problem. There was a long crack all the way down a supportive concrete wall. It didn't take a professional to see that the crack was a danger to the foundation of the whole house. We walked away from that house with heavy hearts. It was a discouraging feeling. We had waited so long and now we weren't sure if it was even going to happen. We knew one thing though. *There was no way we could move forward with a home that had a broken foundation.*

The second house, at first glance, was rough. Instead of the nice looking exterior like the last house, this one was brown all over. The kitchen had the oldest oven I had ever seen, with a gaping hole near the slider door. Critters seemed to think the house was their own personal motel. As we inspected the actual foundation of the home, we were shocked. Structurally everything was sound. The ceilings were smooth with no visible cracks. The house was the size and layout we wanted. It just needed some love. *It needed us.* The inspection came back clean and we rejoiced! We purchased the fixer upper with confidence and very happy hearts. Now we're in the process of changing it into our dream home.

You see, on the surface, the first house seemed like the best choice. It *looked* better by comparison but underneath it was falling apart. However, the second house had a great structure. All the gross interior stuff could be changed with hard work. None of those things were deal breakers for us because we knew the important thing was a good, solid foundation.

"Bow down thine ear to me; deliver me speedily: be thou my strong rock, for an house of defence to save me. For thou art my rock and my fortress; therefore for thy name's sake lead me, and guide me."
(Psalm 31:2-3)

What is our influence going to do when it reaches someone? How we influence other people should go beyond the surface. It's not about how it looks on the outside. If our influence is rooted in the truth provided by The Lord Jesus Christ, it will encourage good behavior and actions. Our foundation in God should be solid or one day it might take down everyone we influence. A good foundation is needed for our protection but most importantly for our connection to the Master Builder. If our influence is not stable, we foster negativity and no matter how sincere we are, we leave others vulnerable to the influence of the enemy.

"Be sober, be vigilant; because your adversary the devil, as a roaring lion, walketh about, seeking whom he may devour"

(1 Peter 5:8)

Our adversary would love nothing more than to see us fail. To trip us up and keep us from God. The foundation for our Christian walk needs to be solid in truth. It can't survive on sandy feel good vibes. God's Word has to be active in our lives or down the road it will be revealed that there is a crack in our foundation. I want us all to make it to Heaven together some day. To get there, it is time to reveal the truths about our foundations.

The enemy knows how powerful we are. Do we?

There is a reason the enemy is not leaving us alone. We belong to Jesus & he knows if he can get our eyes on something else, then we become powerless in our thinking. There is no doubt that we will face trials. *Sometimes it's due to our own foolishness.* Other times its the enemy at work. We are told to be aware and to be discerning but we are only human. Eve's sin brought major consequences that we still face today. God allowed the enemy to make the journey of this life more difficult. *Not to hurt us but to train us through the trials.* The Almighty has all the power but let's things happen anyway. God at the same time reassures us that we would be victorious against the battle if we endure and stay strong in Him.

"And the LORD God said unto the serpent, Because thou hast done this, thou art cursed above all cattle, and above every beast of the field; upon thy belly shalt thou go, and dust shalt thou eat all the days of thy life: And I will put enmity between thee and the woman, and between thy seed and her seed; it shall bruise thy head, and thou shalt bruise his heel."

(Genesis 3:14-15)

My pastor made a statement that touched my heart. It was along the lines of *"a heel wound is painful, but a head wound is fatal."* Do you want to hear something encouraging? God knew back in the garden the battles you would face today. He has assigned power to us through His grace that not only will He be with us through those difficult moments, but we have the power to give the enemy the fatal blow! We also have been given the ability to turn to God in our own wickedness to receive forgiveness.

The time is now to look with a pure vision.

We must humble ourselves to His will for us to experience the fullness of our calling. Whatever baggage we carry, whatever trials we go through and whatever cracks are seen in our foundations, God can take care of everything! We must trust Him. This world is dying every day. To walk around with broken foundations is a death sentence. Doing "Gods" work without consulting God is a dangerous game. Broken foundations spread influence around like a stagnant sprinkler. It may look nourishing to the eyes but the minute it's digested, sickness starts. *We need to want more of Him.* He desires for us to seek His face and know Him. He wants to have daily conversations with us. The Lord Jesus Christ wants us to be a fountain of free-flowing water, tapped into Him at all times! Our foundation should be based upon Him. Nothing less.

"Therefore thus saith the Lord GOD, Behold, I lay in Zion for a foundation a stone, a tried stone, a precious corner stone, a sure foundation: he that believeth shall not make haste."

(Isaiah 28:16)

One word can reach thousands. One message can grab hold of someone who was on the brink of giving up. How is it that One God became One man and died One time, and yet His love never dies? God is alive. That's how. Our influence in this ever-changing world can reach farther than we know. It's contagious. *It spreads like glitter*. If we touch one life, that person can touch another life. It might not be within the same time or even decade.

Living in society today, especially with social media at our fingertips, it's easy to feel rushed. Like we have to "catch up" or we'll get left behind. Through technology, we feel connections with people we have never met in real life. It can be an amazing thing. On the other hand, we are so involved with the lives of other people that we seem to forget that they are real people! We are tempted to respond with harsh feelings. Perhaps because we're not face-to-face, we visualize an invisible shield that's protecting our identity. I feel that God is speaking to us right now saying:

"Listen. I have set a solid foundation. I care about you enough not to leave you without one. Trust me and use it! It is sure. It is unmovable. It is tried and precious. Please do not be hasty and miss out on your blessing. I have what you need. Take it!"

God-ordained influence never expires. It is everlasting.

The Lord Jesus Christ has perfect love. There are no flaws or blemishes. It is not twisted. It is not perverted. It is not smoke and mirrors. God's love is the real deal. We won't find any cracks in it. If we miss out on His love, it's because we haven't allowed it to perfect or correct us. We can choose to let Calvary move us towards growth or let our souls join the fate of fear on that hill. *Foundations matter.* The amazing thing about God's perfect love is that it is unstoppable and can do the impossible!

"We love him, because he first loved us."

(1 John 4:19)

Calvary wasn't based on God's warm fuzzy feeling about you and me. He wants a relationship with us and to give an opportunity to make Him the Lord of our hearts. *To be known.* Love is not an emotion. Love is an act of the will. When the Bible says that we are loved, it's not to glorify how great we are. Obviously, it makes us feel great, but we shouldn't act like that's the reason *why* He loves us. It shouldn't puff us up. We are loved because He *first* loved us.

His love speaks volumes about His Character. There is nothing compared to it. It lacks nothing. When He demonstrated His love for His creation on Calvary, that action was unmatched. It was pure in motive, mighty in power and accomplished exactly what He said it would do. *We're not enough but Jesus is.* God's love is perfect. It is constant. It is faithful. Unwavering. Unshakable. Human beings are fickle. Fragile. Emotional. Made of bones, marrow and flesh.

Comparing His love with the love we see is nonsense.

There is nothing greater than the love of Jesus. Our hearts must trust in Him, believe in the Identity that God has given us about who He is and know it without wavering.

"Trust in the LORD with all thine heart; and lean not unto thine own understanding. In all thy ways acknowledge him, and he shall direct thy paths. Be not wise in thine own eyes: fear the LORD, and depart from evil. It shall be health to thy navel, and marrow to thy bones."

(Proverbs 3:5-8)

A solid foundation doesn't make things sway. If the foundation is a rock, it should be strong enough to withstand any winds of uncertainty and confusion blowing by. Houses built on concrete are more durable than houses built on sandy beaches. Our foundations can't depend on tiny particles of soft material to hold up the structure. We can't afford to labor for years only to have the house collapse. (Matthew 7:26) *There will be casualties.*

When God commanded us to love each other, He meant we need to act it out with thoughtfulness. Making sure our foundation in Christ is founded on the right principles and motives. That is part of the action. Our foundation will dictate the stability of our structures in our Christian walk. The influence we have on others around us will stem from the strength of our foundation. *We are responsible for how we influence their lives as soon as we invite them to partake in a relationship with us.* We should want our influence on our friends and family to promote the solid love of the Savior. Anything else can lead to destruction.

"I know thy works, that thou art neither cold nor hot: I would thou wert cold or hot.
So then because thou art lukewarm, and neither cold nor hot, I will spue thee out of my mouth."
(Revelation 3:15-16)

Being lukewarm will not save this modern world. It won't make a difference because there's not much of a contrast. When God made light, it was different than darkness. *It had to be.* The very basis of who we are in Christ must be different than who the world wants us to be. This is what I saw in myself. My foundation wasn't steady because I wasn't pursing God with everything I had. The Lord was trying to reach me with His transforming power but I only allowed myself to get slightly touched by it. Just enough to get by.

Too many of us are lukewarm today. To have one foot in and one foot out in this climate of society is tragic. We have, more than ever, plenty of resources and opportunities to shine for the Lord. To shimmer for His glory. A half-Christian life isn't enough to move mountains. It's not enough to make a dent in the hard shell of change. I understand we're not responsible for saving everybody. That's God's job. But we are called according to His purpose and when we aren't "all in", ready to do what He's instructed, the world won't take us seriously with any messages we try to bring. This needs to be serious to us. It can't just be a casual fling with God. It needs to be the real deal. Our relationship with God has to have active love. It can't just be one sided. No relationship can work well that way. That's not the way God wants it either. If He wanted half-hearted commitment, Jesus wouldn't have fully committed to Calvary. *What if He never went through with it and decided it wasn't worth it?* When we don't follow through with our part in this relationship between creation and Creator, that's what we're saying to God. That it wasn't worth it. *We aren't worth it.*

Being lukewarm says that Calvary didn't matter.

Being indecisive is a decision. We're choosing what's comfortable. Not too hot and not too cold. Just right for sin to develop and grace to fizzle. While we are sitting in our comfy cocoon of lukewarm faith, God's trying to get our attention. He wants us to know that we are worth it! Worth every slash that His back endured. Worth every drop of blood that dripped from His brow. Worth every aching muscle that stretched out on that cross. We need to have our worth rooted in Jesus. That's the only way we can be somebody who changes the world. That's the only way God can change us.

We want to test the waters of Christianity and keep the comforts of the world.

Would you be interested in someone who was not fully committed to you? Would you be satisfied if someone wanted you but also wanted somebody else? A relationship can't be established without both feet in one place. There is no place for confusion when we know the King of kings. Confusion is when we're choosing to stay at a crossroads instead of picking which path to go on. We need to choose the path that leads to God's love! On that path, chains break off weary feet. Broken hearts are made whole. Scattered minds gain clarity. Anxiety goes running. Fear flees. *The path that leads to the Lord is not always easy, but the benefits have eternal rewards.* We shouldn't be interested in just testing the waters. Dipping one toe into the church to see if it's worth diving in. Let me tell you friend, it is so worth it!

"For God is not the author of confusion, but of peace, as in all churches of the saints."
1 Corinthians 14:33

When I came to God 11 years ago, I was a hot mess. I lived a life of being cold towards God for so long, it corrupted my thinking. Soon the Lord started working on me and though it was a beautiful beginning, I still didn't understand that I was given the opportunity to have a deeper relationship with Him. I became lukewarm for a while by not committing myself completely to God. It all changed when I started to see Him for who He was. A loving and merciful God, ready to forgive no matter how filthy my sin was. Willing to hold His dirty daughter and wipe her angry tears. Tenderly speaking straight to my core and revealing life-giving truth.

I chose to be in this fully because God chose to fully invest in me.

I'm not here to test the waters. *I'm here to be immersed by it.* I want to be fully covered by the water, fully submerged in it. I want to be so far into Jesus that I can't even get one foot out of the water and onto dry land because I would be too far away from shore! There is a peace and a calm that comes with being all in. Even when the storms of this life continue to rage, we won't be tossed about like a lukewarm boat. Not sure if we want to stay on the "safe" shore or adventure out. There's nothing safe about being lukewarm. If God doesn't like the taste of it, then we can't be it. We need to be more than that. We should have an elevated mindset. *God's love should be enough to convince us to run to Him, open arms and willing heart.* We need to start getting real with the Lord who made us. We can't hide from God. We are only deceiving ourselves and trying to pull our worth from things and people that don't matter as much.

"Who shall separate us from the love of Christ? shall tribulation, or distress, or persecution, or famine, or nakedness, or peril, or sword? As it is written, For thy sake we are killed all the day long; we are accounted as sheep for the slaughter. Nay, in all these things we are more than conquerors through him that loved us.

For I am persuaded, that neither death, nor life, nor angels, nor principalities, nor powers, nor things present, nor things to come, Nor height, nor depth, nor any other creature, shall be able to separate us from the love of God, which is in Christ Jesus our Lord."
(Romans 8:35-39)

These verses list a lot of things that can't separate us from the love of God. *However, one thing that can be the biggest wedge in receiving it is our own selves.* We can choose to be separated. We can choose to not love God back. We can choose to stay lukewarm. *Let's not do that.* Let's rise up and claim our worth in Jesus! No more half-hearted commitments. It's time to go all in, fully surrendered to the changing power of God. The battles that keep chasing us in circles can be conquered. The lies that keep running through our minds can finally be silenced forever. The influences in our lives that hinder growth can be cut off and the raw edge of sin can be smoothed out by grace.

Be persuaded that His love will never run out on you like other people have.

Being lukewarm is a lack of trust in God. That is the bottom line. We don't trust Him enough to do what He has promised, and we don't trust that His power is enough to save us. Maybe we have been hurt too many times by people in our lives that we feel tapped out. Our trust tank is empty, and we don't see how the Lord is different from them. We're still clutching our fears like they're a shield that protects our hearts. The reality is it's pushing the Healer away.

God is the Rock. He is strong and mighty. There is nothing that can break Him. *If our foundation is in Jesus, we cannot be broken.* We are protected in the Rock. When we are lukewarm, we're not fully protected and are exposed. Holding our fears as a shield doesn't protect us at all. The enemy is attacking and we're being wounded because of our indecisive mentality. I don't want to be vulnerable to the devices of the enemy again, so I protect myself by abiding in the Rock. When we have His word hidden within us, we have power from the Rock to stand on. We can stand firmly on the Rock of our Salvation. When the winds of trouble come to blow us over, we know who we can rely on to keep us strong and safe.

Scripture are the written words spoken from the heart of the Rock.

Growing up Catholic, our Bible studies were different than the Bible studies I have now. We weren't given Bibles to take home. They were sacred and stayed at the church. I can remember as a little girl wondering why I couldn't take such a special book home to read. I was always intrigued and wanted to learn more. As I grew up,

I still had that desire to know more about the Bible. Even when I was rebellious, I needed to know the truth for myself. When I finally had my own Bible in my early twenties, it was a precious treasure to me! It was also intimating. There were many funny sounding words and numbers. *I didn't even know where to begin.* But once I started reading the Bible on my own, God started to work on my heart. He filled in so many gaps that had been open for years. He answered questions I never knew I had. The spiritual pieces to the puzzle were connecting and truth was unlocking. I was convinced that the Holy Bible was in fact God's written words. The Lord influenced men of God to write down His spoken words and stamp them forever in ink.

We can carry it around wherever we go. Now, we can download the Bible to an app on our cellphones. As technology evolves, it has become easier to access information whenever we need it. This now includes carrying the written word of God! Right in our pockets all day, ready to help whenever we need it, available any minute of any day. *There is no excuse big enough not to use it.* We could take five or ten minutes to open the Bible app and read. We don't always need three hour blocks of morning time to get deep Bible study in. Where is that innocent curiosity to know more about God? Have we lost it as we've aged? I fear the more knowledge we've gained in earthly things makes us feel so smart that we don't think we need the Bible to tell us anything. However to compare man's thinking to God's is not possible.

Our greatest intelligence doesn't even touch His.

He will always be greater than we make Him out to be. *We can never out-learn God.* Which is why we need to decide to follow Him and trust that He knows what to do. Our very foundation will not stand apart from God. Digging deep into knowing Him is what will start the mending of the cracks under the surfaces of our hearts. Having an awestruck reverence to the Word is what will continue to strengthen the foundation under our feet. *Continual communion met with continual devotion.* That's how we're going to make a difference. That's how our influence will channel His influence. I'm done being lukewarm in my relationship with God. *It's time to heal my cracked foundation.* Pray with me:

Lord,

You have shown Your love in a mighty way and I don't feel worthy to receive it. Help me to take the necessary steps closer to You. Whatever is trying to hold me back from Your arms, I rebuke it. I no longer choose to be lukewarm in my faith. Revive my revelation of who You are. Bring me to a place of repentance because that's where change starts. Please heal the foundation that I have and seal the cracks that sin has pierced within me. Show me who You are in the midst of this trial. Teach me to remember my worth in you. In Jesus' Name, Amen.

4

Trees

Growing up in beautiful New England, I had a special tree I would climb. I loved climbing trees. It had the perfect spot on a branch for me to sit with a good book or with my trusty notepad. Journaling was therapeutic and allowed me to escape into my imagination. I would read or write up there, overlooking our yard. My sister and I even gave it a nickname. We called the tree "Given" because we both felt the tree gave us so much. Whenever I visit with my own children, Given is still standing strong. It's branches blowing in the breeze, as if it is waving hello to an old dear friend.

Have you ever thought what life would be like without trees? There wouldn't be any life. Trees produce the oxygen we breathe and reduces the amount of carbon dioxide in the air. They provide shelter to animals. Many different types of food grow on trees as well. If we didn't have trees, the environment and economy would suffer greatly. If we look at trees in a spiritual way, the Bible references them often in scripture. Trees are used as a physical example to parallel the Christian life.

"The Spirit of the Lord GOD is upon me; because the LORD hath anointed me to preach good tidings unto the meek; he hath sent me to bind up the brokenhearted, to proclaim liberty to the captives, and the opening of the prison to them that are bound; To proclaim the acceptable year of the LORD, and the day of vengeance of our God; to comfort all that mourn; To appoint unto them that mourn in Zion, to give unto them beauty for ashes, the oil of joy for mourning, the garment of praise for the spirit of heaviness; that they might be called trees of righteousness, the planting of the LORD, that he might be glorified."

(Isaiah 61:1-3)

We're given a closer look at what it means to be "trees of righteousness" in these passages. To become "trees of righteousness", there must be an exchange. We must repent and let go of what hinders us so that God can replace it with something better. We can be sturdy, rooted people who shine forth the goodness of God. This will ultimately glorify the King and accomplish His will. Anything opposite of that is like a shrub, a stout immature tree. We're not called to be shrubs. We're called to be trees; a walking symbol of strength, resilience and nourishment. Other people will look at our transformed lives and notice a different root system. They should see a difference within us. They should see righteousness.

We're called to be higher than where we are.

"And what agreement hath the temple of God with idols? for ye are the temple of the living God; as God hath said, I will dwell in them, and walk in them; and I will be their God, and they shall be my people. Wherefore come out from among them, and be ye separate, saith the Lord, and touch not the unclean thing; and I will receive you, And will be a Father unto you, and ye shall be my sons and daughters, saith the Lord Almighty."

(2 Corinthians 6:16-18)

Hopefully when we meet other people, they will see God in and through us. My hope is that people will be encouraged to follow God too. Maybe my lifestyle and how I carry myself can plant a seed; a desire to have a similar life for themselves. A life rooted in God and flourishing good fruit! *We should live so that we inspire others to crave a positive change.* To trade in the struggles for triumphs. Old ways for new paths. Hope when everything seems hopeless.

God uses trees as a symbol for what we must be like.

I'm reminded of the "trees of righteousness" in my own spiritual life. Pillars in the church. Men and women who are completely sold out to God regardless of their past. Those who have paved the way for the younger generation. Even if I don't have close relationships with everyone, their presence in service reminds me of their sacrifice and dedication to the things of the Lord. *Firmly planted. Resilient. Brave.*

We need to understand there is a reason why our elders hang onto the lifestyle and morals established long ago. Whether it's how to behave in a respectful manner around people of the opposite sex or the importance of personal prayer, our elders see why we must continue honoring those same principles. If the church is to be a part of revival in this modern day, we need to be extra cautious how we use our influence. *Just because the generations before us didn't have smart phones, doesn't mean they're not smart!* It would be wise for us to listen and yield to what our elders are trying to teach us. Their influence is the reason why we are here and have a thriving movement. God has used them to help correct and instill the principles that He has designed for His people.

The legacy of righteousness will outlast the flash-in-the-pan touch of the prideful.

Technology has come a long way in the 11 years since I've been in church. It has changed the way we get up every day and get ready. The beeps of notifications that catches our attention regardless of what's going on. An alarm, a text, a reminder, a sale, a like. *Look at me! Look at me!* I feel they scream without really having to scream. We are more entertained and distracted than ever before. Our elders had their own things to deal with and nothing was easy back then. Every generation has to deal with challenges. *We have to come at technology with the right spirit or we'll be consumed with the wrong ones.* This is true when we look at some of our services and altars. *When our bass is bumping so loud we can't even focus on what God is saying, there's a problem.* There's a price we will pay to stay relevant. We were not called to be the same but set apart. If we want our influence to make a difference in a positive way, we have to stop trying to do it all alone, in our own prideful strength. Every moment we ignore the Godly wisdom of an elder, we could be missing a soul that needs to be won. *That soul might even be our own.*

If we are full of ourselves, we can't be full of Jesus.

There is only room for one to be glorified. When we put ourselves on a pedestal, we leave no room for God to dwell. Not because He can't but because it is against His will. Yes, we are called higher, but we cannot climb up there by our own might. *There is not enough talent or gifts in us that will bring us up to the level that God has for us.* He has to appoint us to that position. We can't claw our way up without His leading. Our pride is our downfall. We have so much technology at our fingertips and knowledge accessible in an instant. Any subject, at any time. In whatever language we want. This knowledge is great but without God, it can lead to puffed up pride.

This will make it difficult for us to receive godly council from those in leadership positions. *We think we know it all, so we don't have to listen to our elders.* This attitude needs to change if we want God to be glorified. There's a reason why Paul says in his letter to the Corinthian church that he must "die daily". Paul knew that in order to fulfill the will of God, he had to empty himself first.

We are not God, so it is only fair that we stop acting as though we are gods and expecting people to worship us for the things we do. There is only One God and His name holds more power than all our names put together. The Lord Jesus Christ deserves the glory alone. *If our mission is not to elevate Christ in every situation, then we are at enmity with Him.* I know that if I go by my own emotions, that my influence will only foster negativity.

Wrong motives will never birth right results.

God has no equals. We can't act like we're on the same level as He is. The Lord's knowledge and wisdom is untouchable. The only way to tap into it is if He gives it to us. *And He does.* Just a taste through His Word, through preaching and through elders. This is why we also can't act as though we're on the same level as our elders. *We are not.* They paid their dues and have sacrificed so much to get to where they are. They dug their roots when situations and people tried to pluck them out. The ground was prepared for them, seeds planted, and they grew up to be mature Christians. Faithful saints. *Trees of righteousness.* To change the atmosphere of the church with spiritual oxygen that we can benefit from.

The spirit of entitlement has no business in the ministry or in Christianity as a whole. If we want to help build the Kingdom and influence those around us like

Christ did, we must crucify our flesh first. We must follow the examples of our elders.

"Knowledge puffeth up, but charity edifieth."
(1 Corinthians 8:1)

It is not a popular concept. It never was. As each generation grows up in the faith, they come to a cross road: serve God or serve self. To pick up their cross and follow Jesus or try to live on their own without Him. Spoiler alert: there's no guarantee the second way will ever work. The way to the top is not up. You must lay pride down before God will put you on a mountain top. *We have to humble our hearts and seek His face.* We must be diligent in seeking the Lord every day, reading His Word and adopting a genuine attitude of prayer. If we are not, we not only miss out on our generation's potential, but we are taking away from the next generation's power of influence.

"Humble yourselves in the sight of the Lord, and he shall lift you up."
(James 4:10)

We must ask ourselves honest questions to achieve greatness without an expectation of rewards or accolades. The only thing we need to do is kneel and thank the One who gave us the opportunities we have. He paid the price for us. God doesn't owe us anything and nobody else owes us anything either. *We can't witness to a dying world with an entitlement mentality.* It will silence our voices. What we want might look good on the outside and cause some emotions to stir. That's okay. We can desire good things. It's how we go about attaining them that shows the state of our heart. That will dictate our influence in this world. At the end of our life if we have not exercised His fullness within us and have laid down our agenda, God will call out our prideful spirits.

Zeal sounds good but it'll never work like anointing.

I get it. We have great ideas and are so full of zeal. Dude, I get excited too! Like jump on the sofa, scream in a pillow excited. I love a good idea and have had my share of them. *The error occurs when we are so focused on being a leader of great things that we undermine the great leaders who came before us.* Those saints who have paced the prayer room floors for victory and shedding late night tears for revival. "Trees of righteousness" who attend services faithfully, clean the bathrooms, sweep the kitchen and bring their grandchildren to Sunday School. *The Glitter Effect is alive through their testimonies.* Influence fueled by the love they have for their Creator and the passion to pursue His will. We must take inventory of the countless blessings they have deposited into our legacy. It's the only way we will be able to pass the torch to the next generation after us.

Everybody wants to be a preacher but not everybody is called to be a preacher. You don't need a pulpit to preach. Our influence takes on many forms and every member of the body is important to the Kingdom. We should always tread carefully around those who claim this calling. If we are preaching the Word of God but we haven't sacrificed anything for it, we should be cautious of what our messages convey. Sacrifice leads to heart changing experiences. Comfort leads to self-gratification.

To be anointed is to be tried in the fire. And survive.

If you want an anointing, then get ready because the storm is coming. The storm will be designed by the

Master, to allow real life to teach you. Then you will be able to help others get through the same thing with God. *The storm will only be tempting if there's a sin within you that God is trying to pull out.* Trees don't grow overnight. It takes a long time for a tree to be mature enough to start sprouting branches, leaves and fruit. We see people established and flourishing and we want to jump ahead, skip the important lessons and rush life. That's not how it works. The ministry you end up with would be sickening to the body. *You need to want God more than you want the calling.* He will equip you with everything you need if you wait on Him.

"Wherefore let him that thinketh he standeth take heed lest he fall. There hath no temptation taken you but such as is common to man: but God is faithful, who will not suffer you to be tempted above that ye are able; but will with the temptation also make a way to escape, that ye may be able to bear it."

(1 Corinthians 10:12-13)

We will have opportunities come up that will test our commitment. *The trials that will come at us have the ability to uproot us from our foundation.* The enemy will attack a sore spot at the core of our flesh. It will be something we have a hard time saying no to. Our struggles won't magically disappear. Everyone struggles with different sins but only God can deliver us from them all! Before we desire to be like our elders and thrive in righteousness, we must go through the purification process. What you hold internally will influence everyone around you in some form. God is giving you this time to be delivered from temptations that can devour your future influence. Don't rush through the process!

We should say this prayer every day:

> *"Lord, if I have anything in me that will hinder or distract the hearts in need of you, then I rebuke that spirit. Empty me now, God. I cannot afford to wait another minute to get right with you. Guide me as I lean on Your Word and mold me accordingly, so that I may become a pillar of spiritual strength in the church. Take up full capacity in my life and have your way now and in the future. In Jesus' name, Amen."*

We were made to glorify The Lord Jesus Christ. To tell people who He is. To spread His truth like glitter. We must strive to be "trees of righteousness" to those little ones looking on. To the next generation. One of our goals shouldn't just be to fulfill the call of God now. *It should be to become a strong elder in the church.* What a privilege that would be! It's no wonder God used trees as physical symbols for the thriving Christian life. Trees are beautiful creations.

"Blessed is the man that walketh not in the counsel of the ungodly, nor standeth in the way of sinners, nor sitteth in the seat of the scornful. But his delight is in the law of the LORD; and in his law doth he meditate day and night. And he shall be like a tree planted by the rivers of water, that bringeth forth his fruit in his season; his leaf also shall not wither; and whatsoever he doeth shall prosper. The ungodly are not so: but are like the chaff which the wind driveth away. Therefore the ungodly shall not stand in the judgment, nor sinners in the congregation of the righteous. For the LORD knoweth the way of the righteous: but the way of the ungodly shall perish."

(Psalm 1)

I must confess. Psalm 1 is my all-time favorite chapter. It has been a lifeline during times when I wanted to give up. I've wanted to throw in the towel on this journey so many times, but I was always drawn back to Psalm 1. The Lord started showing me a hard truth in the last few years. If I gave up on my Christian walk, my witness goes with it. *If I gave into temptations, my testimony is silenced.* If I fall, the eyes of my children, nephews, nieces, and siblings will watch me like a tree being cut down in the woods. Have you ever stood on the ground when a tree falls? *The earth shakes.* I had to look past my own emotions and remind myself who was watching. *I had to focus on being influenced by God so I could be a positive influence to others.* I needed to take my focus off the situation and onto the purpose of why I was placed here. That's how influence works.

In Psalms 1, it paints a beautiful illustration of what the outcome of a person's life should be if they delight in the Lord daily. They'll "be like a tree." The more I researched into how real trees thrive, the more fascinating this verse became. An article published in 1989 entitled "Tree Roots: Facts and Fallacies" by Thomas O. Perry summarizes the importance of a tree's solid foundation:

"Root growth is essentially opportunistic in its timing and its orientation. It takes place whenever and wherever the environment provides the water, oxygen, minerals, support, and warmth necessary for growth."

The growth of a tree's roots depends on where the resources are for survival. They will move towards a source of nourishment. Tree roots are strong so they can stand. It is said that the higher the tree is, the longer the root system is. Just like the foundation of a house is the most important beginning to a structure, the roots are the key to healthy long-lasting trees.

Psalm 1 is saying that if we delight and meditate on the things of the Lord and His instructions, we will be rooted in righteousness. *We will be strong in faith.* We will be unmovable. We will be nourished and thriving. However, we are also warned that if our hearts are not rooted in the right things, it can wither away. A healthy relationship with the Lord will provide all that we need everyday. Just like tree roots, our spiritual roots must seek the right spiritual "water, oxygen, minerals, support and warmth necessary for growth."

Our relationship with God must be rooted in the right soil.

Summer is coming to an end where I live right now. The air is turning crisp and the leaves will soon change colors. A different season means there will be a transformation in nature, especially among the trees. Beautiful warm hues will be painted throughout the leaves. It's a breathtaking sight. I love the warm weather, but fall is too gorgeous to ignore. Leaves are like little factories where food for the tree is produced. They hold special chemicals and nutrients. As daylight and temperatures outside change, leaves are affected and causes the colors to change. While we enjoy the outside appearance of the tree, God has created a wonderful working system within it. A tree can stand strong regardless of the season change.

Our spiritual root system must be planted in the truth.

All that we do and say is but a speck of glitter. We'll have spectators watching us as the seasons of life change. If we want to be helpful to someone else, we must have the right root system flowing within us so that we have the right nutrients to create change. We cannot feed others if we are not fed the right things ourselves. *Neither of us will survive.*

This is a struggle for me. As a wife of one hard working husband and a mother of two sweet but very active boys, being the only girl in the house can be challenging. I'm constantly reminding myself that what I say and do creates the temperature of the home. I once heard during a ladies conference that the woman is the thermometer and the barometer. Our attitudes and actions affect the feeling in the atmosphere.

"Hope deferred maketh the heart sick: but when desire cometh, it is a tree of life."

(Proverbs 13:12)

The word *deferred* is defined as "postponed" and the word *desire* means for "longing." Scripture is telling us that when we postpone hope or encouragement, it can make a heart ill. At the same time when the encouragement the heart longs for arrives, it is a stable life-giving pillar.

"Blessed is the man that trusteth in the LORD, and whose hope the LORD is. For he shall be as a tree planted by the waters, and that spreadeth out her roots by the river, and shall not see when heat cometh, but her leaf shall be green; and shall not be careful in the year of drought, neither shall cease from yielding fruit. The heart is deceitful above all things, and desperately wicked: who can know it?"

(Jeremiah 17:8-9)

Our influence goes beyond the people close to us. It goes through them. They in turn can influence others. *This is Glitter Effect in a nutshell.* People long for hope. This is why it's easy for us to attach ourselves to the wrong ideas or to people who aren't the best influences. *If we sense just a small sliver of hope from negative sources, we allow it to overcome common sense.* "Trees of righteousness" is to consistently have an avenue to the appropriate water source, the Lord Jesus Christ! Tap into the Source. He knows how to nourish you. The thing that holds us back isn't going to last forever if we're willing to hand it over. Trust Him! God is not bound by time and is ahead paving the way. Endure the process. One day the victory will be so much sweeter!

Our prayers are in the hands of a future-knowing God.

To be like a tree, it doesn't end with a root system. *That is only the beginning.* We must also store those nutrients inside of ourselves as we prepare for the proper way to distribute them, much like a tree trunk. If our spiritual roots are in Christ and we are soaking up His Word, those life-giving nutrients must be stored internally before we can begin to share them with others.

The more trees that we have in the world, the richer our air quality. Trees create the right air necessary for other things to live. Without trees, the air would be so polluted that nothing would be able to survive for very long. Carbon dioxide would reign and life on earth would be gone! If carbon dioxide levels are too high, it replaces oxygen and can cause us to suffocate. Scary but it makes a lot of sense. *Trees are life-giving organisms.* God created them to purify the atmosphere. If we start losing too many trees, we start losing our resource for clean, pure oxygen. *We will lose our lifeline.*

Our emotions affect those we're connected to daily.

This message started off for me and then the Lord opened doors for me to share it with others. I'm always struggling with taking the time to allow God to check my spirit when negative feelings arise. *I know how I feel will influence how I act and that will influence my family.* I'm a ball of emotional flesh with a smile most days. One thing we try to do at home is frequent worship sessions. I can sense the change in the atmosphere when that happens. Our focus is no longer on ourselves. *It is shifted to something greater.* Bitterness, unforgiveness and self-loathing are stagnant waters. If we are to be trees, we need a free-flowing current.

It's not just a praise session. It's an intervention.

The enemy would love nothing more than to cut down the "trees of righteousness." He will use every ounce of influence he has to suffocate our revelation of Jesus. If we are plugged into the Lord daily, we'll be able to withstand the harsh winds of evil. God will use us to produce the right atmosphere for survival. This spirit of influence is good fruit that can branch out to the next generation and beyond.

"And these are they which are sown on good ground; such as hear the word, and receive it, and bring forth fruit, some thirtyfold, some sixty, and some an hundred. And he said unto them, Is a candle brought to be put under a bushel, or under a bed? and not to be set on a candlestick? For there is nothing hid, which shall not be manifested; neither was any thing kept secret, but that it should come abroad. If any man have ears to hear, let him hear."

(Mark 4:20-23)

5

Sinkholes

In 2007, I had just started attending church. My boyfriend (and now husband) Jonathan would pick me up every Sunday. My work schedule only allowed time for me to make one service, so Jonathan made sure I would make it. Life was changing and even though it was exciting, it was also scary. I was facing some tough spiritual battles. One in particular was my choices in entertainment. I had not changed the movies and music I was listening to, even though I was attending church regularly. It didn't take long for me to feel a deep conviction about what I was watching and listening to. Soon I started to have a reoccurring dream and I believe it was partially due to the influences I was allowing to entertain my heart.

It was an old house. I stood at the bottom of a dark staircase. The floor boards creaked as I ascended the steps slowly and cautiously. I didn't want to be there but I kept walking up the stairs. My conscience said to turn back but I didn't. As I neared the top of the landing, I saw double doors in the hallway to my left. Beyond those doors was the attic. My hands shook as I stared at the door knobs, which pulsated as the doors breathed, shifting in and out like a heaving chest. I didn't want to open them. Ghastly sounds echoed from the other side. The longer I stood in front of the doors, the more I could feel the air getting hotter. There was no doubt about it. Hell was waiting in there and the devil was waiting for me.

This is a hard story to tell and an even harder message to deliver. It hits close to home for me and that's why speaking about it is challenging. This is also why it needs to be told. If we are always sharing the good things that happen in life, we miss out on connecting with others through our struggles.

Our experiences teach us and we then can help others.

That being said, I wanted to provide some important statistics to reflect on before diving into this hard conversation. An article published by the Western Journal of Medicine, written by Enid Gruber and Joel W. Grube, provided these very insightful facts. *It stated that 80% of young people report that their friends or classmates find out about sex, drugs and violence from entertainment sources.* Their studies report that young ladies are choosing television programs with sexual content more than young boys. Boys, however, are more likely to watch inappropriate movies and listen to music with explicit lyrics. About 60% of music videos portray sexual feelings, perverse emotions and impulses. They display provocative clothing and suggestive body movements. This has been taken to a deeply promiscuous level just in the last decade.

On average, teenage viewers see 143 incidents of sexual behavior on network television at prime time each week and many of those are between unmarried partners. This is just what they're watching on TV. It doesn't include content from social media.

In 2017, it was reported that 73% of 13-17 years old own a smart phone. In addition, over 75% of texters and social networkers sending messages or photos said that they would *not* want their parents to see the contents. The

Statistic Portal, a site dedicated to sharing accurate statistics with the public, said that in the second quarter of 2018, Netflix had over 130 million subscribers. This number is growing rapidly as the year continues. All these facts point to one obvious thing:

Technology has changed how families are influenced.

We can send or receive emails and messages. Take videos or photos and then share them. Play or record music. Upload or download music. Instant live feeds and real-life streams. Play games, internet research or casual browsing. *Instant gratification is drawing our hearts.*

How technology is influencing us starts in our homes. The *content* in which we are consuming and allowing our family, our children and our hearts to consume is important. It won't take much for us to get roped into sin through technology. The influence of the entertainment industry can cause unrealistic expectations about social interactions, physical attractiveness and distorted opinions about love. Many times we are being fed the identifications of fictional characters and we are struggling to separate fantasy from reality. *Technology can be used as a tool to deceive and distract God's people.*

What you invest in, you ingest in.

What we give our attention to will manifest in some form in our hearts. As a creative person, content affects me greatly and the recurring dream I started to talk about was a product of my lifestyle choices. God has shown me that whatever I watch, read or listen to will influence me. I might not even be aware of what's going on. That's how the enemy works. Subtle. *We're living in a world that has no boundaries for the influence we're consuming.*

"For God hath not given us the spirit of fear; but of power, and of love, and of a sound mind."

(2 Timothy 1:7)

Living in Hartford, CT at a young age, I witnessed a family friend being wheeled out of his house into an ambulance. He was only 15 years old and would never return. This incident began to affect my mental health as I grew up. Around six years old, I had both a fear and a curiosity about death. This increased in my preteen and teenage years when I began writing short stories and poems. There were numerous pages of horror and murder plots. By my early twenties, I was obsessed with crime shows on television, scary movies and gory books. *I was more than infatuated; I was captivated.* At the time I thought I was only entertaining myself but spiritually, I was entertaining the enemy.

What we watch, listen to and read influences us.

A positive or a negative impression is deposited within us. As we walk this narrow road with God, obstacles will come our way. Many of them won't feel like obstacles. This is why we are to be discerning, so we can make the right decisions. It's one thing to be rooted in truth and have a solid foundation. It's another to put that into *action* on a daily basis, especially when it comes to how we choose to entertain ourselves.

Have you ever been in a grocery store and later started humming a song? Even though you weren't focused on the music, it was still in the atmosphere and influenced you with little effort as you strolled through the aisles. It might have been later that day when you realized the music made an impression and now the song is stuck in your head!

Negative influences are obvious to us, most of the time. We can detect the majority of them. We might make a conscience effort to avoid them. Subtle influences are different because they can be personalized. Subtle influences may vary between believers and their own relationship with the Lord Jesus Christ. They can be harder to point out. Our spiritual eyes often do not see the danger.

"Be sober, be vigilant; because your adversary the devil, as a roaring lion, walketh about, seeking whom he may devour."

(1 Peter 5:8)

We are allowing ourselves to be deceived by the entertainment industry. Nothing is ever "just a book", "just a movie" or "just a song." There are subtle influences working to distract us from the promises of God. We must compare signs, wonders and visions with the Word of God. The enemy is at work and we're wrapped up in what looks "okay" or "not-that-bad." *Satan wants to make God's people powerless.* The only way he can achieve that is by bringing things to our attention that appeals to our flesh.

If our focus is shifted, the power is shifted also.

If you love God and want to do the right thing, you are in opposition of darkness. *Be awake.* What we entertain ourselves with will work through us and create the atmosphere from which our homes are built. Whatever data we've been consuming will come out in some way. It could be unpleasant attitudes, backward thinking or lack of compassion for others. We must take careful inventory on what goes in and out of our internal influence bank.

If we're in Christ, what we invest in should be elevated.

If God was sitting next to you on the sofa, would He be pleased? If He drove with you to work and heard the music you've had on repeat, would He be delighted? Just imagine the Lord glancing over your shoulder as you text a friend, leave a social media comment or flip pages in the book you're currently reading. Would He proclaim well done?

"Beloved, believe not every spirit, but try the spirits whether they are of God: because many false prophets are gone out into the world."

(1 John 4:1)

We as a church have become numb to the enemy's devices. We have placed our eyes on being entertained but have forgotten to "try the spirits" of what we are being entertained by. Yet many times we continue listening to the same ungodly music, watch the same fear-inducing movies and read the same evil-laden books. Each time we submit our hearts to these corruptions, they are creating a mindset devoid of Christ. *Our spiritual focus shifts.* We then no longer are worried about what is right.

We justify what we don't want to give up.

God reminded me of the rich man Jesus spoke to in the Book of Luke. In the scripture, the rich man inquired about eternal life. The Lord Jesus Christ knew this man was brought up in the faith from his youth and confirmed the commandments he needed to continue following. However, the Lord also knew this man loved his possessions and that was where his heart lied. Jesus told the rich man to give all his treasure away to the poor and to follow Him. Instead of a grateful joy, the man's response was one of sorrow. In the man's eyes, Jesus asked for too much. These earthly possessions wasn't something dispensable to the rich man. *He had accustomed himself to a specific lifestyle and therefore grew comfortable in it.* To give up that lifestyle would be death to his fleshly desires and that price was too much to pay.

"Now when Jesus heard these things, he said unto him, Yet lackest thou one thing: sell all that thou hast, and distribute unto the poor, and thou shalt have treasure in heaven: and come, follow me. And when he heard this, he was very sorrowful: for he was very rich."

(Luke 18:22-23)

How would we respond if God asked us to abandon our comfortable lifestyles in the entertainment we surround ourselves with? Would we die to these daily desires or is the price too much to pay? The rich man was sorrowful. He was full of grief and sadness by Jesus' request. It wasn't something he was willing to surrender. I do believe that the rich man loved God. *He just loved his lifestyle more.* It was convenient and comfortable. He was a ruler and saw how the poor lived. To give up wealth and to live like them was not appealing to his heart. The Lord told the rich man to not only give away his riches but to "come, follow me." The rich man was one choice away from complete, personal communion with the Lord and obtaining an eternal promise. *Just one choice away.*

The biggest hurdle of deliverance is pride.

We have completely left God out of the decision-making process when it comes to how we are entertained. We don't want to involve Him in those choices or ask what He thinks. *Perhaps because deep down we already know His answer.* When we walk with the Lord and we have His Spirit dwelling in us, our spiritual conscience taps into His spiritual heart. Often we continue in sin because it's comfortable, even if we know it's wrong. We've normalized it and have allowed ourselves to become distracted and our treasures lie elsewhere instead of in Heaven.

"Lay not up for yourselves treasures upon earth, where moth and rust doth corrupt, and where thieves break through and steal: But lay up for yourselves treasures in heaven, where neither moth nor rust doth corrupt, and where thieves do not break through nor steal: For where your treasure is, there will your heart be also."

(Matthew 6:19-21)

When I think of the word "treasure", I picture gold coins spilling out of an old dusty trunk. The coins have a smooth surface and they glisten like a million stars. They are happily tossed with the most perfect diamonds and gems. To own such treasure would be an honor and might make us feel important. Treasure like this could change a life. The word "treasure" could also be translated as "deposit." Years ago, I used to work as a bank teller. Even though math is my greatest nemesis, I did like learning about the customers and recognized a pattern during their transactions. Many of the people I assisted would deposit the same amount every day or week. A few customers invested in their futures through a savings or money market account but other customers wouldn't deposit anything at all. They wanted all of their money from payday in cash so they could have a good time during the weekend. They were always excited to inform me of their plans and how the money would be spent. I could see their excited eyes widen as I counted the cash back to them. Their minds were already spending each cent before they even left the bank.

Treasures from this earth have no eternal worth.

What is our investment? What do we spend our time and attention on? Where our investment is, that is where our hearts are. In everything we should be diligent in keeping the Lord as the center of our greatest desires. *Investing in our relationship with the Lord Jesus Christ is essential to the structure of our being.* This is the only relationship that will provide a constant flow of nourishment for our spiritual roots, strength for our spiritual growth and good fruit for our spiritual branches. Trees of righteousness have the fear of the Lord as their treasure. This world will turn our fears into chains, but Godly fear will launch us to the mountaintop where we become victorious. Our goal must be Heaven bound!

"The LORD is exalted; for he dwelleth on high: he hath filled Zion with judgment and righteousness. And wisdom and knowledge shall be the stability of thy times, and strength of salvation: the fear of the LORD is his treasure.

(Isaiah 33:5-6)

Have you ever heard of sinkholes? They are big holes that open up without warning and devour whatever is above them. Sinkholes have been in the news for swallowing up trees, houses and sometimes entire neighborhoods. A sinkhole is caused by rot under the surface of the ground. It suddenly appears without warning because it's happening underground, where we cannot see the rot. Cavities form when water erodes in the underlying rock layer. Sinkholes can also be caused by leftover construction debris underground, if it's in a place where people live. *The ground above gives out because the foundation no longer exists.*

What is your spiritual sinkhole? What is eating away at your foundation that one day might swallow you whole? So many motives behind entertainment is to provoke fear. We need to take inventory of our emotions when being entertained by certain movies, television shows, music and books. Do you feel hopeful and full of joy? Or are you scared, frightened to be alone and uneasy when night falls? God has not given us a spirit of fear, intimidation and hopelessness.

We are chosen vessels to carry a portion of our Father.

We've been given the power to choose what we fill ourselves with. If we pour into our minds entertainment that encourages negativity, that is what will come out. However if we pour refreshing and life-giving influences instead, then we can be used in a positive way in someone else's life.

Our hearts will have more compassion towards others. We will have an awareness that a soul is in need. We will be able to see where they are and throw them a safety rope. Your relationship with God can be the very tool that someone else can use to grab onto and be pulled out of their pit.

"If my people, which are called by my name, shall humble themselves, and pray, and seek my face, and turn from their wicked ways; then will I hear from heaven, and will forgive their sin, and will heal their land."
(2 Chronicles 7:14)

One of the biggest struggles young people face today is being accountable for the content they consume. With just one click, data is instantly downloaded right in front of our eyes. Music can be streamed in less than a minute. Books no longer have to be tangible but can be read digitally with the flick of a finger. Technology is a powerful thing and has changed the way our world operates. As the church, we have to navigate this new territory of entertainment with caution. If we desire our land to overcome the spiritual warfare between good and evil, it starts with our daily choices. For healing to come to our land, a humbling within us must take place or our influence might be a hindrance to the revival of souls.

This world doesn't need more people who love God but never live like they do.

The power of influence is in our daily choices. I do feel God is raising a generation of fearless, anointed people who will understand how to properly navigate the social media and entertainment territory. They are soldiers who aren't impressed by contrasting influence but who are creating Godly content, laced in holiness and truth. People who have respect for their heritage and are not ashamed to share about it. These soldiers understand what not to read, listen to or watch. *He is calling and equipping them for such a time as this!*

"If any of you lack wisdom, let him ask of God, that giveth to all men liberally, and upbraideth not; and it shall be given him. But let him ask in faith, nothing wavering. For he that wavereth is like a wave of the sea driven with the wind and tossed. For let not that man think that he shall receive any thing of the Lord. A double minded man is unstable in all his ways."
(James 1:5-8)

This process of being perfected will never end until we go to Heaven. It is long suffering. However the reward is great if we stay the course. Let's not be like the rich man. *Jesus knew his riches were a spiritual sinkhole.* It was consuming him. Before the rich man even approached the Lord with a question, Jesus already had an answer. *Give up your comfortable lifestyle and follow me.* Feeling sorrow didn't save the man because he was more concerned with what he was losing than gaining. The real sorrow is this sad truth, one that the rich man couldn't see. He never realized that in keeping his possessions and turning away from Jesus', he became spiritually poor.

Our eyes have to look higher than earthly pleasures.

No sin is too deep of a sinkhole that God can't fill it. He can restore the rot that's below our surfaces. The first step is to give up whatever He has asked you to, no matter the cost. It could be a simple TV show that could steer your soul off the path. Once you take those steps to let go, the second step is to follow Him. Trust in the Lord, that He can make something new happen for you. He has your best interests in mind and will comfort you through any trial. Lastly, remind yourself that there is a promise waiting in Heaven that is greater than any treasure you can get down here.

"Therefore if any man be in Christ, he is a new creature: old things are passed away; behold, all things are become new."

(2 Corinthians 5:17)

Take inventory of the content you're consuming. Remind yourself of the purpose God has for your life and the Heavenly treasures that await. Here is the awesome ending to the dream I shared and how the Lord used it for His good.

It was only a few months into church when I received the baptism of the Holy Ghost during an altar call at a district service. I was water baptized in Jesus' Name not too long afterward. One night, I started having that recurring dream again, only this time it was different.

I was no longer cautiously walking up the stairs. I was full out running! Gripping the handrails, I made my way up to the attic hallway. I stood in front of those double doors without dread. Grabbing both handles, I pushed the doors wide open. The room was engulfed in light! It was not Hell anymore but Heaven. The light was intense and beautiful beams cascaded across the floor. I could see the outlines of windows but nothing more because the light invaded every inch of the room.

At that very moment, I physically felt in the real world a POP in my body, followed by an overwhelming flood of the presence of the Lord. It felt like I was floating! The light was so bright that it was white. Waking up from that dream, I could feel warm sunlight on my face, only to realize that it was the actual sun shining through the bedroom window. I laid there and cried tears of joy. My fear in God had made me fearless. I was finally free!

6

Well Water

"But whosoever drinketh of the water that I shall give him shall never thirst; but the water that I shall give him shall be in him a well of water springing up into everlasting life."
(John 4:14)

Water is a pure and clean element. We might be able to survive weeks without food but not days without water. It is essential to the system of the human body and we can't function properly without it. *We need water.*

God has a well of water to replenish and satisfy souls.

The water supply provided by the Lord is not a sprinkle or a drop. There is an infinite supply. The water Jesus gives us is always pouring out. His living water is a free fountain and it's made available to us to thrive, for our spiritual roots to be fed abundantly and growth to continue. The Lord Jesus Christ is constantly providing water freely, without stopping, from a heart that is full of mercy and grace.

Distraction is a valuable tool of the enemy to derail our Godly legacy.

If the enemy can get our eyes on something other than the refreshing power of God, he will. He knows the power behind our influence is because of the Lord and he will use distraction as a method to lead us away from the promises God has for us. The simple truth is no one will force us to approach God's nourishing water supply. We must *choose* to have it active within us and flowing through us, not only for our own salvation but so we can leave a Godly legacy for the generations to come.

"In the last day, that great day of the feast, Jesus stood and cried, saying, If any man thirst, let him come unto me, and drink. He that believeth on me, as the scripture hath said, out of his belly shall flow rivers of living water."

(John 7:37-38)

His water will cleanse us and set the tone for the next generation. We need to be a fountain of life, so He can work through us and our influence will be saturated with His goodness. Let us come to His water and drink, not only to quench our thirst but to prevent a future drought in the hearts of the ones watching us.

It's time to drink the water and become a fountain.

This brings me to the story of Abram and Hagar. In their old age, Abram and Sarai had yet to conceive the promised child that the Lord assured them was coming. Their impatience grew until Sarai had an idea. She gave Abram permission to take Hagar, her servant, and have a child with her. Abram yielded to the voice of his wife and a son was born. Sarai regretted the decision and treated Hagar harshly. Heartbroken, Hagar fled. *She found refuge by a fountain.*

"And the angel of the LORD found her by a fountain of water in the wilderness, by the fountain in the way to Shur."
(Genesis 16:7)

The Lord had mercy and compassion on Hagar. He gave her the name "Ishmael" for the baby boy. Ishmael in Hebrew is *yish-maw-ale'; God will hear.* The Lord promised Hagar that her seed will be multiplied. This moment changed her life! The God of Heaven noticed her heart and gave her hope as a scared mother. *By a well, He was there.* The Living Water for her soul and the soul of her son.

"So she called the name of LORD who spoke to her, 'You are 'God who sees, because I have truly seen the one who looks after me.' That is why the spring was called, 'The Well of the Living One who looks after me.'"
(Genesis 16:13-14, ISV)

As the Lord instructed her to do, Hagar then returned to Sarai. Can you imagine the humility? I assume Hagar did not want to do this, but she believed in the Lord and His Word at the well. She had an Advocate. She had a Protector. She had a Provider. Hagar was obedient and faithful. She was a woman who wanted to be a good mother.

Her soul was thirsty and God nourished it.

"As for me, behold, my covenant is with thee, Neither shall thy name any more be called Abram, but thy name shall be Abraham; for a father of many nations have I made thee."
(Genesis 17:4-5)

At 90 years old, The Lord changed Abram's name to Abraham and revealed the great legacy He had planned for the promised son. God also changed Sarai's name to

Sarah, as preparation for the influence she will have through the chosen seed. This did not mean God forgot about Hagar and Ishmael. God also established that Ishmael would be fruitful and blessed.

The first time the actual term "well water" appears in the Bible is in Genesis 21. Hagar will find herself again at another well years after this pivotal moment between her and the Lord. Ishmael was no longer an infant but a growing teenager. In fact, he was about fourteen or slightly older. Sarah is frustrated when Ishmael starts to cause trouble during a ceremony for Isaac, the young promised child. She demands Abram to send both Ishmael and Hagar away. Though Abraham grieved at this request, the Lord told him to follow through and he did. God wanted Abram to trust Him and the promise He had for Ishmael.

"And Sarah saw the son of Hagar the Egyptian, which she had born unto Abraham, mocking. Wherefore she said unto Abraham, Cast out this bondwoman and her son: for the son of this bondwoman shall not be heir with my son, even with Isaac. And the thing was very grievous in Abraham's sight because of his son. And God said unto Abraham, Let it not be grievous in thy sight because of the lad, and because of thy bondwoman; in all that Sarah hath said unto thee, hearken unto her voice; for in Isaac shall thy seed be called. And also of the son of the bondwoman will I make a nation, because he is thy seed. And Abraham rose up early in the morning, and took bread, and a bottle of water, and gave it unto Hagar, putting it on her shoulder, and the child, and sent her away: and she departed, and wandered in the wilderness of Beersheba."
(Genesis 21:9-14)

The water Abraham provided could only last for so long. As they wandered in the wilderness, the water ran out and Ishmael became weak. Hagar placed him under a shrub for shade. His health was failing, and Hagar found her soul feeling dry again. Another heartbreak and moment of desperation. She stayed close by but couldn't bear watching her teenage son pass away. Hagar lifted up her voice and wept, as Ishmael most likely groaned in anguish. Hope was fading. *Ishmael's life could not go on much longer without water.*

"And God heard the voice of the lad; and the angel of God called to Hagar out of heaven, and said unto her, What aileth thee, Hagar? fear not; for God hath heard the voice of the lad where he is. Arise, lift up the lad, and hold him in thine hand; for I will make him a great nation. And God opened her eyes, and she saw a well of water; and she went, and filled the bottle with water, and gave the lad drink."
(Genesis 21:17-19)

Ishmael survived because God provided water.

Our nation is crying out for more believers to tap into God's sustaining water! When our children are too weak or lost to do it on their own, we must always cry out to God for nourishment and pray that our children will receive life-giving water that only the Lord can provide. *We must advocate for them.* We can't give up hope. When our children are older, they will make their own choices and trials will come. We are to show them the way to the fountain of life that is in Jesus.

Hagar felt helpless, so she cried out to her Helper, the One who nourished her when she needed it most. She knew Him and believed that He could do the same for Ishmael. *We need to hold onto hope!* If we can place ourselves in line with God and stay faithful, He'll use our influence to bring water to the thirsty.

His fountain never runs dry and is always overflowing.

You don't have to be a parent to be an influence in the lives of children. I learned this as an aunt before I became a mom. There were about nine children in our family before I had my own. They were all watching, interacting and learning from me. I'm an influence in their lives. We also have a lot of little ones in our church. Sweet, innocent eyes watching as we worship, sing and listen to the preaching. You don't have to be a parent to make a difference in the life of a child. The younger generations are being influenced by how you carry yourself, handle the glitter messes of life and the miraculous victories too.

Your presence alone can make a difference.

The cost of sin is great. We end up cheating the next generation of the chance to drink from the well. When we aren't tapped into the Source, the well runs dry and there's no water to give to the children. Without a well of water, their thirst will draw them away, to fill that need with other things. Things opposite of what God wants them to digest. Why have generations of believers fallen away from the truth? *There was a lack of water supply.* Children will ultimately make their own choices, even if we do our best but we must continually keep pointing them towards the direction of the water source.

Advocating for the children of His church should be a priority. We must believe the best outcome will happen if we're faithful to the Lord Jesus Christ. Never stop praying deliverance prayers just because you don't physically see a miracle. God works inside our hearts. We need to start believing that our prayers matter because the Lord is faithful and trustworthy. People are fickle, but God is our solid rock.

Jesus is our living water and He can do the impossible.

We can't afford to be a stagnant fountain. *Stagnant water produces deadly bacteria.* I'm sure that well of water in the wilderness God revealed to Hagar was sitting a while. Maybe the water smelled as the bacteria broke down whatever living organisms were left. In that moment, however, Hagar didn't think twice to reach down and pull up the water. It might not have been clean but God was involved. Hagar wasn't concerned about the state of that motionless well water.

She remembered her God and her safety lied in Him.

We can't survive with the water we've been holding onto for days, weeks or even years. We need to constantly be tapped into His free-flowing fountain, otherwise we are left with stagnant water to feed our children and the result is as messy as a glitter spill. The lives attached to ours might end up looking at the scattered pieces and following every shiny lead. The next generation might have no idea that there is a water source to go to. The fountain is waiting but they've become too busy filling their buckets with everything else.

The danger of the church is an abandoned well.

Stagnant water is a host to disgusting and often deadly parasites and bacteria. It is motionless and isn't nourishing to the human body. It's not flowing or moving. It's just sitting. It can be as small as water in a bucket or as big as a lake. The size doesn't matter because the similarities don't change. Aside from health risks, there are environmental risks. Stagnant water can be dangerous to the world we live in. It can happen anywhere. *In our own homes. In our local church. In our hearts.*

Motionless water is low in oxygen. It isn't healthy for us to consume. When water is moving, it is pulling in oxygen that is consumed by fish or other animals that live in water. *In stagnant water, no movement means the oxygen cannot be replenished.* Isn't that amazing? When God created this earth, He made sure everything had a purpose and that everything worked together in a great powerful system! He could have created us with all our needs tapped out and never needing to be restored but He didn't. *We still need oxygen, food and water.* We still need to consume elements to be sustained and to grow.

"He maketh me to lie down in green pastures: he leadeth me beside the still waters. He restoreth my soul: he leadeth me in the paths of righteousness for his name's sake."
(Psalm 23:2-3)

Still waters can be different than stagnant waters. In this verse, "still" means "quiet" or "peaceful." David is saying that the Lord is leading him to a land that is flourishing with nourishment and the water he's near is tranquil. In that place of peace with God, David's soul is restored, and he is led down a path that is full of righteousness.

The quiet places with God is what will restore our soul.

    The Lord has declared many promises to His children in the Word. He is faithful to complete them, but We still need to do our part. *God has given us a responsibility to be a wholesome influence.* David wasn't perfect but what makes his story great is that he didn't sit stagnant in sin forever. He no longer tried to get by with just a little bit of God. *He got closer.* The closer David got to God, the more peace he found and eventually David was a fountain full of flowing water! The Lord flowed through David like a mighty, moving water source as he penned beautiful poetry and insight. If David had been content with stale water, history would be different. He knew God could sustain him and God knew David could influence us today.

    God is our Living Water and His Word has enough spiritual nutrients to change us into who He has called us to be. We need His never-ending, never-failing water supply!

7
Crossfire

As we read in the last chapter, Hagar returned to Sarah when the Lord told her to, despite the hurt she must have felt. She also departed without protest when Abraham sent her and Ishmael away. *Hagar submitted herself to the authorities in her life and she was blessed for it.* The scripture doesn't speak of any foul words shouted from her lips. There is no record of Hagar being disrespectful. Instead, she was humble and meek. Her meekness didn't discount her heartbreak, but it helped in her healing. Meekness is gentleness.

"The meek shall eat and be satisfied: they shall praise the LORD that seek him: your heart shall live for ever. " (Psalms 22:26)

Hagar's submission to the Lord and the authorities in her life is an example for us today. Today, many people don't want leadership. We desire complete independence to do and say what we want without consequences. We naturally don't want to submit when someone else is in charge. Having full control is satisfying to us. Listening to someone else give instructions can feel confining. Adapting to change initiated by another person can stir up prideful resistance. Submission is a lost art and our influence is fading with it.

Submitting to the authorities over you is respecting their position given by God.

How would Hagar's story played out if she didn't go back to Sarah's house after the Lord told her to? Yes, she was brokenhearted and sorrowful. Hagar had emotions like any other person. Emotions have a purpose but often we allow them to lead us. However, the Lord will not be glorified if our emotions are magnified. Our emotions can't be trusted. *When we don't submit to the Lord, there will be a cost.* Maybe we won't see the consequences in the natural but spiritually our disobedience will hinder the work God wants to do within us.

Submission can change the course of our legacy.

We never know how our submission to God can touch the ones we love. If the Lord has instructed us to do something and we choose not to, what example is that for the next generation of believers? For those young eyes that watch us. *Delayed obedience to the Lord is still disobedience.* The Almighty has chosen to make Himself known to us and wants a personal relationship. We must trust that God knows what He is doing, and we are to obey Him. There's a popular song on the radio that I love. The lyrics are a beautiful poem of woven words that illustrates a heart willing to obey the Creator. One portion sings:

"If the stars were made to worship so will I
If the mountains bow in reverence so will I
If the oceans roar Your greatness so will I
For if everything exists to lift You high so will I
If the wind goes where You send it so will I
If the rocks cry out in silence so will I
If the sum of all our praises still falls shy
Then we'll sing again a hundred billion times"
- *Hillsong, So Will I*

All creation outside of human nature yields to the Lord. The wind goes where He sends it. The oceans, rivers and streams all follow a glorious system designed for a magnificent purpose. Animals follow their wired instincts. The entire galaxy does what God has created it to do. The whole universe works within those boundaries because it's a great, flawless system. *Disobeying the Lord and spiritual authorities is not trusting in the Creator.*

"Seek ye the Lord while he may be found, call ye upon him while he is near: Let the wicked forsake his way, and the unrighteous man his thoughts: and let him return unto the Lord, and he will have mercy upon him; and to our God, for he will abundantly pardon. For my thoughts are not your thoughts, neither are your ways my ways, saith the Lord. For as the heavens are higher than the earth, so are my ways higher than your ways, and my thoughts than your thoughts."
(Isaiah 55:6-9)

My son David is fascinated with the story of Jonah. To a young boy, it's pretty awesome that a man gets swallowed by a giant fish! At the same time, he relates personally to the way Jonah disobeys God's orders and runs away. Jonah's actions and choices are still being discussed today. *The Glitter Effect!* Could Jonah even predict how one choice would be written down and retold generations later? Of course not. Yet here we are, reading what happened and learning from it. His influence is active right now, just as much as it was active back then. Let's read his story from the beginning.

"Now the word of the LORD came unto Jonah the son of Amittai, saying, Arise, go to Nineveh, that great city, and cry against it; for their wickedness is come up before me.

But Jonah rose up to flee unto Tarshish from the presence of the LORD, and went down to Joppa; and he found a ship going to Tarshish: so he paid the fare thereof, and went down into it, to go with them unto Tarshish from the presence of the LORD."
(Jonah 1:1-3)

Within the first few verses of the story, Jonah already has to pay a cost for disobeying the Lord. He literally has to pay money as he tries to run away. God gave him specific instructions to witness to the people of Nineveh and Jonah in that moment had two choices; He could submit to the Lord and obey or not. Jonah wasn't concerned about the spiritual needs of the people of Nineveh. So he tried to run and hide.

"But the LORD sent out a great wind into the sea, and there was a mighty tempest in the sea, so that the ship was like to be broken. Then the mariners were afraid, and cried every man unto his god, and cast forth the wares that were in the ship into the sea, to lighten it of them. But Jonah was gone down into the sides of the ship; and he lay and was fast asleep."
(Jonah 1:4-5)

On a battlefield, crossfire is when a line of gunfire from opposite sides cross. It's the meeting point of conflict. Sometimes this word is used when people are having a disagreement between one another. Crossfire in both instances can harm innocent bystanders who are led into the meeting point or unknowingly walk right in the middle of it. By fleeing God and boarding that ship, Jonah led the mariners right into the crossfire of his own spiritual battle. When Jonah made the decision to board the ship, his choice to disobey will affect everyone on it. The Lord sent out a powerful wind and all of the people on the boat were now in danger. All because of the choice of one man. *Crossfire.*

Be aware who stands in the crossfire of our conflicts.

The sailors became afraid. They didn't know what to do, so they called after their false gods as the storm raged. Their prayers didn't work, and the boat started breaking apart. *God was sending Jonah a powerful message.* He was giving Jonah an opportunity to cry out to Him and repent. Jonah doesn't submit and instead decides to rest, falling asleep inside the ship. The scripture gives no mention that Jonah was concerned about the lives of the innocent sailors on board. He doesn't seem to care one bit that everyone was panicking, crying out to false gods, when he knew the real God.

"So the shipmaster came to him, and said unto him, What meanest thou, O sleeper? arise, call upon thy God, if so be that God will think upon us, that we perish not.'"
(Jonah 1:6)

Jonah continues in his disobedience, despite of the fact that other people were now caught up in the crossfire of his choices. Eventually the captain wakes up Jonah because everyone is crying out to their gods except for him. The captain tells Jonah to do the same, in hopes that they will survive this horrific storm in the middle of the sea. However, it doesn't take long before the truth is revealed to the scared sailors. *Jonah was part of the problem.*

"And they said every one to his fellow, Come, and let us cast lots, that we may know for whose cause this evil is upon us. So they cast lots, and the lot fell upon Jonah. Then said they unto him, Tell us, we pray thee, for whose cause this evil is upon us; What is thine occupation? and whence comest thou? what is thy country? and of what people art thou? And he said unto them, I am an Hebrew; and I fear the LORD, the God of heaven, which hath made the sea and the dry land."
(Jonah 1:7-9)

This is the first time Jonah acknowledges who he is and who the Lord is. This confession is the beginning of freedom from the wrestling emotions within Jonah. Admitting his identity and the Identity of God takes integrity. I wonder if, after hearing every sailor trying to reach gods that don't exist, Jonah felt this was his opportunity to share with them. One interesting observation is how the mariners became afraid after hearing Jonah's confession

Jonah's crossfire with God endangered the sailors.

His conflict put everyone in physical danger as the hurricane winds almost demolished the ship. Jonah's choice to flee because of fear caused fear to rise up in the hearts of the mariners. Jonah had questioned if God would truly deliver the people of Nineveh if he obeyed and preached to them. Jonah lacked trust in the Lord. He allowed his own emotions to guide his path and that affected other people.

Submission requires denying yourself.
Disobedience requires denying God.

Jonah's disobedience was no longer his issue alone. As the story goes on, he suggests that the men throw him overboard to save themselves. This was the beginning of repentance within Jonah. The sailors really didn't want to do it. They even tried rowing harder, but the storm was too great. Then something amazing happened! The same men who called out to false gods, turned their hearts and cried out to the Lord. *Idolaters began to understand the truth about God.* At this point, Jonah had yet to utter a word to the Lord about the situation, but the sailors pleaded in prayer before throwing Jonah into the chaotic sea. As his body plunged into the water, the waves became calm. What a confirmation that there is only One God and He heard the men's prayer! They responded with reverence and made promises to the Lord. At the end of the entire ordeal, God was glorified!

"And he said unto them, Take me up, and cast me forth into the sea; so shall the sea be calm unto you: for I know that for my sake this great tempest is upon you. Nevertheless the men rowed hard to bring it to the land; but they could not: for the sea wrought, and was tempestuous against them. Wherefore they cried unto the LORD, and said, We beseech thee, O LORD, we beseech thee, let us not perish for this man's life, and lay not upon us innocent blood: for thou, O LORD, hast done as it pleased thee. So they took up Jonah, and cast him forth into the sea: and the sea ceased from her raging. Then the men feared the LORD exceedingly, and offered a sacrifice unto the LORD, and made vows."
(Jonah 1:12-16)

I don't believe at this point of the story that Jonah had enough faith in the Lord. I'm convinced he was sacrificing himself and ready to perish out of guilt. God wasn't caught by surprise when they threw Jonah overboard. *God knew the events that would unfold.* He knew what was in Jonah's heart. When the Lord brings us to a place where we're staring into the deep end of our trials, we can either fear drowning or trust that He has prepared a way of escape.

"There hath no temptation taken you but such as is common to man: but God is faithful, who will not suffer you to be tempted above that ye are able; but will with the temptation also make a way to escape, that ye may be able to bear it."

(1 Corinthians 10:13)

God had prepared a great fish to swallow Jonah and save him from drowning. The Lord already had a plan in place. Jonah was led to prayer and repentance in that fish belly. The Lord again commanded Jonah to go preach to Nineveh and this time he obeyed. *Jonah was ready to fulfill his calling.* There was still work that needed to be done in that stubborn heart of his, but Jonah became a great prophet and will forever be known as the chosen vessel used to save the Ninevites from destruction.

The Glitter Effect works positively and negatively.

When Jonah boarded the boat filled with innocent sailors, his choice brought a consequence that could have ended very deadly. However, in the third chapter, Jonah obeys God and tells the people of Nineveh the message from the Lord. His submission to the Authority above brought fruition to the Kingdom of God! The king listened to Jonah and was pricked in his heart. The people listened to the king and were pricked in their hearts. Everyone understood the message that the prophet received from the Lord. The story of Jonah is an amazing example of the power of our influence through our choices. The influence we have can either elevate fear or shine His light.

When our choices line up with His will, that's when miracles are born.

8
Good Fruit

It's easy for us to focus on the disobedience in Jonah's story but I believe it's also a message of hope, especially for us who are following God and are trying to grow in Christ daily. *If we allow ourselves to fully trust God, He will come through!* The Lord is good, honest and holy. God is powerful and can use our influence to bring good to the world.

"Wherefore lay apart all filthiness and superfluity of naughtiness, and receive with meekness the engrafted word, which is able to save your souls. But be ye doers of the word, and not hearers only, deceiving your own selves."
(James 1:21-22)

When Jonah repented and submitted himself to the Lord, lives were changed. His life, the lives of the sailors and the Ninevites all experienced change because Jonah decided that God's way was the best way. *Jonah became a tree of righteousness.* Now many years later, he serves as an example for us today. He wasn't perfect but when he noticed how his choices were affecting others, he stopped fighting God and instead started following God. At the end of the story, Jonah helped produce good fruit. He just had to listen and follow through.

The difference between a dreamer and a doer is the follow through.

I remember the first time I wanted to become a professional artist. I was eight years old and having fun drawing in art class. It was great. My teacher Ms. Giardi was so patient and kind. She took the time with each student to make them feel important. When she noticed my growing interest in art, she said to practice more. It was a short chat but opened my understanding greatly.

Practice isn't about perfection but about progression.

If you want to get better, you have to do the work. We are all called to do great things for the Kingdom. What we fail at remembering is that growth should happen during our every day living. To practice better discipline, self-control, patience and submission. To practice what we've learned through Bible studies and preaching. To practice being a follower of the Lord Jesus Christ in every moment, regardless of how we feel. To practice loving others.

Many times, we have this vision of how we want to be in Christ. *We put it on a pedestal like an idol and admire it from afar.* It's as if we don't think we can attain that level of obedience to God. In that oppressive mindset, our awareness of our influence is shut down. Thankfully, the Lord has provided Biblical examples of people who have made it. People who have given themselves fully to the Lord, no matter what their pasts looked like.

God's heart desires for no one to perish but to thrive.

"Being confident of this very thing, that he which hath begun a good work in you will perform it until the day of Jesus Christ."
(Philippians 1:6)

It's not the will of God for us to permanently fail. He knows we will stumble but the Lord doesn't want us to stay down. God has provided the tools for us to grow spiritually by His definition. We must move past the thought that once we fail, there are no more options. *There is always an option.* God will never leave you without a life preserver, even if it comes in the form of a large, stinky fish! The Lord of all creation takes a personal interest in us and never desires us to be without help.

His Word is consistent in equipping you with everything needed to get back up and try again.

When God created a tree, He was intentional. It was crafted with purpose and from the roots to the branches, everything worked according to a system to provide fruit. If fruit could not be produced, it meant there was an issue with the system. There must be a lack of nutrients to make the tree healthy. It would be considered a dead tree, only good for chopping down into logs and making firewood.

"Bring forth therefore fruits worthy of repentance, and begin not to say within yourselves, We have Abraham to our father: for I say unto you, That God is able of these stones to raise up children unto Abraham. And now also the axe is laid unto the root of the trees: every tree therefore which bringeth not forth good fruit is hewn down, and cast into the fire."
(Luke 3:8-9)

Good fruit begins by having a good foundation. When our spiritual roots aren't grounded in God, we are deprived of the necessary nutrients needed to be healthy trees of righteousness. If we are spiritually unhealthy, we won't produce good fruit and therefore are in danger. Jonah was spiritually fruitless until he focused on God and stepped into the role that waited for him.

"Every tree that bringeth not forth good fruit is hewn down, and cast into the fire."
(Matthew 7:19)

Jonah was close to being cast down for good, but God provided a chance for the story to end differently. When he surrendered fully to the Lord's calling, Jonah's influence brought fruition and salvation to the people of Nineveh. This story encourages us to look at God first and follow Him. What He has in store is greater than anything we can ever imagine for ourselves.

Our vision should line up with His vision for us.

God has called us to be trees of righteousness. I imagine this as being tall, firm, full and flourishing. We won't blow over when the wind comes because we will be established in God so deeply. Perhaps we'll be like waving flags of victory, standing side by side as a great army of faithful pillars. The Lord wants us to be alive in Him, with His living water flowing through us just like a tree. *In God, we can have healthy branches that will bring forth high quality fruit.* This will be on display like a glorious crown for all to see! How we present ourselves will represent the God we serve.

Be an example that will provoke the next generation to rise up higher.

It's not God's will for us to become firewood. We are to become spiritually healthy people who can be used to spread the gospel. The truth is, it's hard to feed others without good fruit. What good is a tree that keeps producing rotten fruit or no fruit at all? If a person keeps choosing to disobey God, they'll only produce fruit that is inedible or nonexistent. That person might speak distastefully and encourage the things of the world more than the things of God. *His living water isn't flowing through them.* They don't have a stable foundation and could be a danger to themselves and other people. If one tree in the middle of the forest starts leaning too far, it's only a matter of time before it breaks. When God takes an axe, He doesn't want to do it maliciously, but He is protecting those who are still standing strong. It's better that one perish than the destruction of many.

Good fruit is anything that pleases God and has the ability to feed others.

Our daily walk with the Lord should speak about who God is. Your personal relationship and commitment to Jesus is the best witness to others. You may not need to utter a single word about God because people notice how you carry yourself. Whether it's by your character or your clothing, they see a difference in you compared to what they're used to seeing in the world. We should be so far into God that when people see us, they will have no doubt who we follow. One way to do this is how we dress ourselves.

"Either make the tree good, and his fruit good; or else make the tree corrupt, and his fruit corrupt: for the tree is known by his fruit."
(Matthew 12:33)

Years ago, I made the choice to stop wearing pants. It was a personal decision and it shocked those who knew me for a while. God had laid this conviction on my heart during individual Bible study time and through preaching at church. It became clear to me that what I wore was important to God (Deuteronomy 22:5) The choice to only wear skirts and dresses led to conflict in a few of my relationships. A childhood friend made an accusation that insinuated I was easily manipulated and gullible. It was insulting. Many people also hinted at brainwashing, all because I didn't want to wear pants anymore.

In my mind, switching the clothing I wore was a minimal change in comparison to the bigger picture. I had experienced a life altering revelation about the Lord so in my mind, giving up a piece of clothing was a reasonable sacrifice. Honestly, I didn't realize how it would affect others though. *What I had chosen to do was going against the normal mindset of the world.* This experience taught me that we don't have to speak a word for people to be impacted by the choices we make, no matter how personal they may be.

Our influence has power just by our presence.

Eleven years later and modesty is trending in the fashion industry. Who would have thought? Regardless if society thinks it's acceptable, what we do needs to be acceptable to Jesus only. Yielding to holy conviction will lead to producing good fruit within us. We have the opportunity to follow God in the midst of opposition. When we stand firm in our convictions, it's noble and an example of righteousness. We can't control how people react to our choices but we must continually follow through, giving God the glory.

Modesty and holiness should clothe our hearts too.

When we are modest within, we'll be able to exhibit modesty in our wardrobe. Modesty gives us freedom from vain thoughts and having a prideful spirit. What we say, how we treat other people and carry ourselves should be based on His standards. *Modesty is not "hot." Modesty is holiness.* It is sacred and should be the mirror in which we reflect the goodness of our God. We will shine like glitter for His glory, instead of staying dim. Holiness is a beautiful, sacrificial calling in the life of every Christian. As a lady, one of the privileges I have is to share my relationship with the Lord through how I dress. It is a banner that waves boldly in a society that runs on perversion and rebellion. God performed a miracle in my heart and it's an honor to reflect that outwardly.

"Cleanse first that which is within the cup and platter, that the outside of them may be clean also."
(Matthew 23:26)

Modesty shouldn't make us feel captive. We should not feel begrudged to look different. This is a visual age we live in. The power of our influence is magnified more than ever. We are visually stimulated every day and it's important what image we're portraying. If God looked at your social media photos and private text conversations, would He see a modest heart? In order to please God, He may require us to make a choice internally, that will reflect outwardly. *Good fruit is defined by a good God.*

Modesty isn't a product of shame, but a robe of holiness.

Our Father is the King of kings and He has specific expectations for His daughters. Let Him use you to be a light, clothed in dignity. There will be voices encouraging you to "show it all" and celebrate your body by wearing less. *However, in order to make a difference, we have to be different!* Good seeds must be planted in our hearts and minds before good fruit can be produced through us.

When I think about allowing God to determine the standards for a modest lifestyle, I'm encouraged by the story of Esther. Before Esther became queen, she had to go through a process of preparation. As we look more into the details of her story, we will see that God gives Esther wisdom in how she should dress and conduct herself around the king. While the other ladies chose what they wanted, Esther had a different mindset which set her apart from the rest.

"On the seventh day, when the heart of the king was merry with wine, he commanded Mehuman, Biztha, Harbona, Bigtha, and Abagtha, Zethar, and Carcas, the seven chamberlains that served in the presence of Ahasuerus the king, to bring Vashti the queen before the king with the crown royal, to shew the people and the princes her beauty: for she was fair to look on. But the queen Vashti refused to come at the king's commandment by his chamberlains: therefore was the king very wroth, and his anger burned in him."
(Esther 1:10-12)

King Ahasuerus wanted to showcase Queen Vashti's natural beauty to the people of the kingdom, but she refused and dismissed the invitation. This made king Ahasuerus very upset. It was a serious offence, especially in those days, for anyone to deny an invitation from the king. It was also humiliating coming from another member of the royal family. *Queen Vashti disobeyed direct orders from the king, but more than that, she denied the king himself.* Not accepting the invitation was a jab at his position, their marriage and status in society. The king felt he had no choice but to release Vashti of her crown. She will no longer be queen.

"So it came to pass, when the king's commandment and his decree was heard, and when many maidens were gathered together unto Shushan the palace, to the custody of Hegai, that Esther was brought also unto the king's house, to the custody of Hegai, keeper of the women." (Esther 2:8)

    The search for a new queen began for king Ahasuerus. Every young unmarried woman in the land was brought to the palace to stay. This included an orphaned Jewish girl named Esther. She had been raised like a daughter by her older cousin Mordecai, a palace worker. When Esther arrived, he walked the courts every day to check on her well being. Mordecai was fearful that Esther would be punished for being Jewish, so he forbade her to speak of it. He loved her and wanted to protect her.

    For the next twelve months, the women at the palace went through a customary process of purification. This usually focused on pampering themselves with oils and perfumes. It wasn't all for vanity. Many of the people in those days suffered from skin diseases and different illnesses. This lengthy time-frame was to prevent any unclean health issue from entering the king's house and affecting him. This year was to prepare them for meeting the king face-to-face. It was also enough time that a woman's true character would be known.

When the year was done, it was time for the king to meet with each potential bride. Every woman was given the choice to use whatever they wanted in the palace to adorn themselves to appease the king. This could have included decorative jewelry, elaborate hairstyles or beautifully tailored clothing. What was worn depended on what the woman decided. There was one wholesome Jewish girl, however, who used her power of choice differently. Esther wanted to know exactly what the king would like. There was the overseeing officer named Hegai who worked closely with the king. He had years of experience and knowledge that would bring Esther a better perspective on how to please the king. She allowed Hegai to choose something to the king's satisfaction before her meeting with king Ahasuerus.

"Now when the turn of Esther, the daughter of Abihail the uncle of Mordecai, who had taken her for his daughter, was come to go in unto the king, she required nothing but what Hegai the king's chamberlain, the keeper of the women, appointed. And Esther obtained favour in the sight of all them that looked upon her. So Esther was taken unto king Ahasuerus into his house royal in the tenth month, which is the month Tebeth, in the seventh year of his reign. And the king loved Esther above all the women, and she obtained grace and favour in his sight more than all the virgins; so that he set the royal crown upon her head, and made her queen instead of Vashti."
(Esther 2:15-18)

I believe the king was impressed by what Esther wore and the condition of her heart. There is a difference between "appease" and "please." While the other women wanted to *appease* the king, Esther wanted to *please*. To "appease" is to pacify with a quick solution, by giving or saying something to fulfill the request, need or person. It's the giver interpreting how to satisfy the receiver.

While appease isn't a wrong action, please is an action with purpose. To "please" is to unselfishly be intentional with how to fulfill the request or need that will benefit the receiver. Esther was being purposeful when she allowed Hegai to choose how she should be presented to the king. While everyone else had their own ideas about what the king desired, Esther wanted the truth.

Purposeful choices are essential to pleasing the Lord.

What if Esther followed the trends of the other women? Would she have been chosen as queen? From the moment she arrived, Esther was purposeful with her choices. Her influence in the kingdom became a great force in the deliverance of the Jewish people. Esther's cousin Mordecai found favor after he revealed a murder plot against the king's life, shortly after Esther became queen. When the time came to uncover the wicked plans against the Jews led by Haman, Esther's place had been prepared. She stepped in humbly and informed the king of Haman's evil intentions to destroy her people.

Esther was no longer afraid to speak about who she was, a Jewish woman. She had gained not only the favor of the king but his full trust. He knew her heart and character. The king gave the orders and Haman was hanged, freeing the Jewish people from his disastrous plot. Mordecai was then placed in a leadership position and became one of the greatest advocates for his people.

"For wisdom is better than rubies; and all the things that may be desired are not to be compared to it."
(Proverbs 8:11)

No matter what society is doing, do what is right in the eyes of our King! The influence we've been given can be used to glorify the Lord if we just aim to please Him and will lead to good fruit for the next generation. How we represent God outwardly should reflect the changes He has made within and encourage other to rise their standards to a more holy expectation.

9
Reflection

Eve walked along the beautiful garden with a heart full of thanksgiving. Her fingers danced off the surrounding greenery, as her eyes thoughtfully glanced at every branch and all the fruit that He had provided. Her soul sang a thousand songs and her spirit dwelt in peace. Her bare feet softly strolled through the blissful green grass, as her nose twitched to the smell of Paradise.

She continued strolling through Eden until a whisper awakened from the shadows. The subtle serpent convinced her that Paradise was not enough and that she could be like God. Her gaze no longer looked upon everything around her as a blessing. There was a shift in perspective. She now viewed the world as something smaller. She looked at the forbidden tree and saw a different story from the one that was told to her. Plucking the sweet fruit off the branches, she could almost taste it before her mouth was open and as she bit into the flesh, the veil fell off from her eyes. Paradise no longer looked appealing but instead looked like prison. With an outstretched hand, Eve shared the fruit with Adam, who took it without hesitation. Together they noticed a dynamic change, towards their surroundings and each other. They noticed their exposed state. Together they became fearful of the Lord and so they hid.

One choice can start a generational chain reaction.

One thread that ties the stories in the Bible together, is that an action can change the course of history. The decision in the heart of a woman completely overpowered the common sense in the mind of a man. Influence can be a gift or a curse. The choice is made in the hands of the influencer. What looked shiny and beautiful on the outside, held unmistakable sin inside. Satisfaction was not fulfilled the way Eve thought it would be. It only took a whisper from the serpent to turn her eyes away from a loving God and onto seeking more outside of Him. *Sin within our hearts never just affects us.* Eve's sin brought consequences to her life and Adam's. It ejected them from Paradise and thus brought a curse upon mankind.

Eve devoured the fruit and sin devoured her.

This storytelling brain of mine can't help but be curious about the plan God had for Adam and Eve before they sinned in the garden. Of course, He knew they would choose to disobey even before they decided it. But what if they didn't? What if at the very last moment, before Eve's tongue touched the skin of that fruit, she stopped? *Just for a second.* Just long enough to remind herself of the graciousness of God and who He has shown Himself to be to her. What if she reflected on the revelation of His Identity? Maybe she would have pulled back from the serpent, widening her eyes in remembrance. I wonder what she would tell herself if she had paused to ponder the situation over:

"*My God isn't keeping anything good from me! He has proven I can trust Him because I don't lack anything. He has provided everything that is necessary to supply my needs and He told me not to eat this fruit, so I don't need it. If my loving Father tells me not to eat it, I won't do it. All my hope is in the Lord and everything I need is within Him. I'm completely satisfied just to be with God. I don't need anything more.*"

God's plans for us are better than our plans for us.

It's too late for Eve's story to be rewritten but we still have time. The stories in the Bible are meant to perfect us, to become the people He wants us to be, to fulfill the potential that is inside of each of us. *That He may be glorified as we are sanctified.* There will be subtle serpents trying to whisper to us, tempting our attention away from what matters. Yet what if we became bold instead of reactive with our choices?

In this modern world that's full of yelling voices desperate to be heard, our voice needs to be different. *Our voice needs to reflect the Good Shepherd.* When people see us, they should be reminded of the Lord we serve, and our influence should inspire them to want to know Him more. To reflect God, we must get to know Him for ourselves, so that He may work within us and eventually through us.

"I am the way, the truth, and the life."
(John 14:6)

The Lord Jesus Christ meant every word of this verse. Whether you're still a new believer or you've been in the game a while, sometimes reading scripture can feel like a chore at times. Our flesh begins fighting back and we find ourselves quickly skimming sentences. It's important to remind ourselves of the grace that is spoken of throughout the Bible.

God didn't have to tell us anything, but He chose to.

When Jesus said "I am," He was setting the foundation for the rest of the message. It has purpose and meaning. When studied deeper, the phrase "I am" connects to the Oneness of God. In Exodus 3:14, the Lord responds to Moses' confused question as to who should he say sent him to free the Israelites out of Egypt.

"And God said unto Moses, I AM THAT I AM: and he said, Thus shalt thou say unto the children of Israel, I AM hath sent me unto you."

This is what Jesus was proclaiming in the New Testament, that He was in fact the "I am"! How amazing is that! He wanted people to know who He was because that is the most important thing. *When we are among different groups of people, they should all know our identity.* We should establish this foundation early in our relationships: that we are a follower of God and in Him we abide.

When it is mentioned that "I am a Christian," most of the time the mood changes. Have you ever experienced this? Curse words become a minimum. Topics are carefully chosen. There are already preconceived notions about what I would tolerate and, to be completely honest, the majority of those notions are correct! *Being open about being a believer sets the tone for the relationships we'll have.* It also leads the way to position ourselves as people they can trust because we were bold and honest.

When we're truthful, it brings opportunity for change.

Our values can't just be something we say. *It needs to be woven into the fabric of who we are.* Truth will always separate the darkness from the light and not everyone needs to be comfortable it. You're not called to make everyone comfortable. In fact, many people did not appreciate Jesus' boldness about who He really was. However, living truthful lives when done properly with His guidance and the right boldness, can bring the words someone needs to hear.

We have to stop worrying so much about what people think when we're living for God. *We need to care more about what God thinks of us.* The people we read about in the Bible were not perfect, but they were willing to be reflections of Him. They came face-to-face with confrontations that made them uncomfortable, especially when it came to their faith. *Truth isn't an easy pill to swallow, but if discarded, it can have life-altering consequences.* We need truth to survive. We need truth to thrive.

If we see truth as an option, we'll never choose it.

Truth should be non-negotiable. That doesn't mean truth hurts less. That doesn't mean truth doesn't require change. Sometimes we are called to shift our focus and attention in order to be aligned with God. *If we are to share the gospel, we must be truthful, so we can be trustworthy.* When an unbeliever looks at our lives, do they see Him? Is our influence a mirror of the Holy One? Have we made the right choices to place God at the center where He belongs? Adam and Eve were made in the image of God but never became the reflections He desired them to be.

If we are willing to become a reflection of the great God we serve, He is gracious enough to make it happen! Eve believed the wrong thing. She believed in a false truth. We must be discerning so we don't believe false truths because they will distort our view of who God is. *God doesn't change but how we view Him can.* Our influence will be tainted with the false truth instead of the absolute truth. The truth that God Himself has already established.

God is exceedingly greater and calls us to greatness.

I want to always choose this truth: God is not vile or evil. He is not boastful, vain, malicious or a liar. God is not a bully, mean girl, gossiper, prideful showman, dramatic actor, or slothful moocher. God is not trying to ruin my life, take something good from me or lead me the wrong way. He is the "I AM." He is "the way". He is "the truth". He is "the life". I will proclaim that He is my God, follow His way, believe in His truth and He will direct my path!

There are a lot of genuine messages out there but genuine doesn't always equal truth. There is a big difference. Truth can cut through darkness while being genuine can't. Truth can break through walls and tear down strongholds. Being genuine is a soft light in the dead of night. You can almost see what's going on, but truth magnifies the clarity of a situation. It opens our understanding and we are able to make better choices. It's okay to start with genuine intent but we should strive to end with solid truth.

People who need Jesus, need us to be His reflection.

If we are to reflect Christ, we need to remind ourselves that we're not better than anyone. We all have sinned, and it is only because of His goodness we are forgiven. Think about the tables Jesus used to sit at to minister. He walked into the homes of the poor more than the religious temples. *Jesus wasn't afraid of being tainted because He knew who He was.* And as much as we want to shake our finger at the sinner and scowl, the Lord makes it clear what the truth really is for us.

"For all have sinned, and come short of the glory of God" (Romans 3:23)

We can't ignore hurting people and expect a revival, and at the same time, we can't have revival without being His reflection. It has been in God's plan all along for our influence to be the light for other people to follow. This means we have to make relationships with those who are hurting, broken, addicted and ashamed. We can still be separate in our beliefs, purpose and knowledge. In fact, we are called to be separate in action and intention.

You don't have to participate in sin to have friends.

The power of God in your life can keep you from getting tainted, as long as your choices remain fixed on Him and His purpose for the situation. You have to be present with them in some way in order for your voice to be heard and for the opportunity to arise to bring them to Jesus. Be a shoulder to cry on and have ears that listen. You can still live for God and be a good friend.

"Wherefore come out from among them, and be ye separate" (2 Corinthians 6:17)

It is a burden of mine to use my influence to build His church and that can only happen if I connect with people outside of it. We often parade around with puffed-up chests, disgusted by the sin of others. We walk past the unsaved with lifted chins, as if we have the power to choose who gets to go into Heaven. How can we know their story if we never speak to them? When we allow God to move through us and we reflect who He is, we can be used to speak about His perfect love.

Give the lost your attention so they may be found.

There is a fear that settles into the mind of a believer at times and it is that we are not to mingle with the unsaved or we will fall. This makes it difficult to create friendships outside of the normal circles of like-minded people. The truth is, being in church doesn't mean they have a good heart. You have to start believing that God will show you the unhealthy hearts who will hinder your Christian walk and that He will prompt you to cut ties with them. This is not a church condition but a heart condition. People who are not in church need to see Jesus in you, but they can't do that if you never meet them. The lost need to understand why we love Jesus so much and we can't tell them if we're only around believers, ignoring the hard conversations. *Hear me: you don't have to hang out with non-church friends wherever they go or do whatever they do.* If you go to school, work, Target or Starbucks then God will open the right doors for you to build relationships with certain people. Those are the opportunities where you can reflect Him.

A good friend will respect your spiritual convictions.

Our focus needs to be elevated above Eve's focus. Let us not be tempted by the whispers of someone who isn't willing to let you live for God. *There is nothing like the power of influence that belongs to a good friend.* It's influence that celebrates light and doesn't cast shade over it. It's the kind of friendship that doesn't cause strife often, isn't jealous much or doesn't look for offenses. We all need friends and sometimes we make foolish choices to have them. As you live this life, you'll find that a handful of truthful friends is better than an army of traitors.

"Then Judas, which betrayed him, answered and said, Master, is it I? He said unto him, Thou hast said."
(Matthew 26:25)

You might have a moment in your life like the moment when Judas betrayed Jesus. He took full advantage of his friend's love and ultimately met his fate when the guilt was too much to bear. Trying to do the right thing in the eyes of the Lord isn't a very popular lifestyle in the world today. People might take you for granted. Opposition isn't fun, but it is within the details of the opposition that God's goodness can be magnified.

"Be not deceived: evil communications corrupt good manners."
(1 Corinthians 15:33)

This begs the big question: can you be friends with sinners and still remain saved? *Yes...but you need to take inventory of the spiritual battlefield on an individual basis.* Jesus was not surprised by the actions of Judas because He knew him. They had spent a lot of time together and Judas' greedy heart was revealed before that moment. Take into account the person's character and their weaknesses. Ask the Lord if there is anything inside that person that will cause you to fall. If you don't feel strong enough spiritually to handle certain people, then step out from those relationships.

Salvation should never be traded in for friendship.

You can't walk on the fence in a lukewarm faith surrounded by unsaved friends. You will fall and be devoured by sin. The strength of your faith cannot waiver if you are to be a witness. We have to be careful around people who will push us over, either carelessly or purposefully. Those are the people that might ignore all your convictions and rush to blow the fire out that God had lit inside of you.

"For God, who commanded the light to shine out of darkness, hath shined in our hearts, to give the light of the knowledge of the glory of God in the face of Jesus Christ."

(2 Corinthians 4:6)

Light is pure and holy. It doesn't dance around trying to please everyone. One way to tell if a person is not a good influence for you is by looking at your moral compass and seeing which way it points when that person is around you. I do believe relationships with unsaved people is essential to the growth of the church. Scripture is full of examples. However, we have to take inventory on how they influence our walk with God and how we influence theirs. We must protect our salvation at all costs. To be saved, we must believe that Jesus is God. We must be baptized in His name and filled with His Spirit. We must live a holy lifestyle, honoring His Word. In addition, we must share what we know with those who don't know.

"Wherefore we receiving a kingdom which cannot be moved, let us have grace, whereby we may serve God acceptably with reverence and godly fear:
For our God is a consuming fire."
(Hebrews 12:28-29)

You want to be friends with unsaved people? Then you have to have His fire lit inside of you at all times! It must be present in a mighty way or you will be quick to look at the darkness as good and forget the vessel He has made you to be. God wants to consume us, working through every part of our being. The friendships on earth shouldn't hinder our eternal inheritance. We should have friends who are willing to foster goodness, humility and forgiveness. Who let us be who we've chosen to be, in Christ. Friends who won't pressure you to harm yourself or to go places that make you uncomfortable. Friends that may not understand spiritual freedom but let you dwell in it!

Heaven isn't full of people who never made mistakes.

Yet, they are filled with people who let God lead their lives. We need to stop trying to form ourselves to something another person likes. Changing our appearance, personalities and even our agendas just to have friends. Look around you! Everything was either created with His hands or the hands of creation. Which one has the power to stand forever? *What God made or what man made?*
We shouldn't fashion ourselves according to what the majority is saying is okay. Our minds need to be settled on who God is and that we will honor that regardless of who we're friend's with. *Renewed thinking leads our*

hearts to diligently pursue purity over popularity. We are a reflection of who we follow and spend our time with. Foster friendships that foster your walk with God. Let Jesus be your Friend first so that He can show you who the rest of your friends should be.

"I beseech you therefore, brethren, by the mercies of God, that ye present your bodies a living sacrifice, holy, acceptable unto God, which is your reasonable service.

And be not conformed to this world: but be ye transformed by the renewing of your mind, that ye may prove what is that good, and acceptable, and perfect, will of God."

(Romans 12:1-2)

10
Pillars

There's a part of me that believes that God knew this life wasn't going to be easy for us. Perhaps that's why He allowed the lives of certain people to be recorded in print, so that we could have examples to help us in our journey. *Our God isn't only the God of now but the God of all time.* He sees things before they occur and that includes the struggles in our lives that haven't happened yet. God has given us examples of men and women who had a relationship with Him, and despite the trials that took place in their lives, they made it through. *Therefore, it is recorded in His Word records of lives changed by a God who cannot change.*

This includes His own flesh story. When Jesus walked the earth, He was tempted in the same ways we are tempted today. He experienced life firsthand. Yet, Jesus did not sin and fulfilled the prophecy to create a new covenant between man and God. His obedience to the cross and sacrifice on Calvary lays a foundation of hope for us, that we can have deep fellowship with God and it will lead us through the temptations. Through the life and death of The Lord Jesus Christ, we are given hope that everything needed to make it through our own Calvary moments, He can provide. Through the example of Jesus, we can better understand the importance of putting God first and how obeying His Word is essential to obtaining everlasting life.

Jesus is a pillar of complete surrender and grace.

Through His example, we are given tools to overcome anything in life today. Jesus' influence didn't only affect the people of His day, but it continues to echo through the generations that followed. We are still impacted by Him in extraordinary ways. Jesus defined true love and mercy. His self-sacrifice continues to revive the hearts of creation and draws people closer. His actions proved His message about love.

The influence that pillars have on us is great. At our fingertips, through His written Word, the Lord gives us examples to look up to for hope. What is a pillar? An object of resilience and strength, that holds up a structure on a solid foundation. As believers, pillars are the people who started their journey before us and always points others to Jesus. Pillars are an example of wisdom, leaving legacies that will continue to bless the generations to come. Pillars are elders and saints who have seen the faithfulness of God and have decided not to be moved.

Pillars roots run deep and are not easily blown over.

As we continue to study and read the Word throughout our walk with God, we'll read about people who didn't feel ready to do what was asked of them to do. *People just like us.* Men and women following God scared, obeying through their nervousness and yielding to His voice even when they didn't feel good enough to be close to Him. God used the broken, the perverted and the ignorant ones to carry out His purpose. He doesn't use the perfect ones. He uses the willing!

God will use the unknown to make Himself known.

Abraham, David, Jonah, Hagar, Esther, these are only a few of the names whose stories were recorded with a purpose. *The Bible is full of great examples of imperfect people being used by a perfect God.* Pillars who laid the foundation so we can connect with the Lord on a deeper level today. Each of their stories are personal and shines light on the state of their hearts. At the same time, we're able to see the true Light work through each person, bringing them through trials and into a beautiful covenant with Him.

"The elders which are among you I exhort, who am also an elder, and a witness of the sufferings of Christ, and also a partaker of the glory that shall be revealed: Feed the flock of God which is among you, taking the oversight thereof, not by constraint, but willingly; not for filthy lucre, but of a ready mind; Neither as being lords over God's heritage, but being ensamples to the flock."
(1 Peter 5:1-3)

When God told Abraham about the legacy to come, he had to learn to trust in the Lord. All Abraham had was God's Word that something good was coming. As the years went by, Abraham made foolish decisions despite knowing God was with him. He fell many times, even with the promise from God on his life. Still that didn't stop God from using Abraham to begin the lineage that changed the world.

"Remove not the ancient landmark, which thy fathers have set."
(Proverbs 22:28)

As the storms of life rolled in and rolled out, the pillar remained standing. Maybe the ground shook a little and the enemy declared battle, but the pillar never gave up and eventually the enemy fled the scene. Hardships and heartbreaks might have brought them to their knees in desperation, but they kept the faith. They followed God and planted themselves firmly in His promise. Pillars are more than strong supports. Pillars are trees of righteousness!

Elders are not a nuisance but our support system.

We wouldn't be where we are without the people of God who persevered, no matter what came their way. The generations before us lived through spiritual famines and droughts. Some lived through wars - physically and spiritually - and survived. The Lord continued to establish them and honored their long suffering. If we take a moment to pause the next time we're in a church service and look around the congregation, there are many pillars still suffering. There are some suffering in silence as the younger generations ignore their fellowship. Pillars who have hearts full of hope, waiting to see the promises of God unfold after all these years. They are waiting to see their prayers answered. *We must be careful how we treat the elders in our church.* They are the reason it still stands. Their influence is a gift to us, not only as an example of righteousness, but as a voice of wisdom.

"Is any sick among you? let him call for the elders of the church; and let them pray over him, anointing him with oil in the name of the Lord: And the prayer of faith shall save the sick, and the Lord shall raise him up; and if he have committed sins, they shall be forgiven him."
(James 5:14-15)

There is a special anointing that God gives the faithful pillars of the church. It is given to those who have soaked the altar carpet with tears of brokenness. The ones who arrive early to pace the floors in travailing prayer, pushing back the gates of hell with their pleas. The people who go home and church is not just a place they leave because it's woven into their identity. *They are the church!* The elders don't have to talk to you or even know your name to have an influence in your life. God uses them to transform the atmosphere of every service.

Elders bring us back to the basics.

Every Sunday and Wednesday night service we have a moment where the time is opened for us to share a testimony. I participate when the Lord places something on my heart, but what I really love is hearing my elders speak. It thrills my soul to hear about elders who should have died but God stepped in, and now are standing up to declare His goodness; hearing about married couples who were once at the brink of giving up but are now praising God for not giving up on them. Soul after soul. Pillar after pillar. Each with a story that brings Him glory!

"But ye are a chosen generation, a royal priesthood, an holy nation, a peculiar people; that ye should shew forth the praises of him who hath called you out of darkness into his marvellous light"
(1 Peter 2:9)

It gives me hope and I'm encouraged by their faithfulness and trust in the Lord. When they share who God is and what He did for them, it reminds me who is in control of this thing called life. At the end of the day, He still reigns! He is the God of miracles. He is the Almighty chain-breaker. He is true love, complete peace, a faithful friend and so much more. The testimonies of our elders are life-breathing opportunities for us to connect with the heart of God.

Change and obedience are great things but without love, we risk being selfish while pursuing the transformation. Without reverencing the Lord, our efforts become self-centered. Scripture says that we are a chosen generation, but we weren't chosen because we are good. We weren't chosen because we know all the answers or are the most talented people ever to walk this earth. No. We were chosen because God is good! His love defines our purpose. We are to be a reflection of His light because He is love. It speaks more about who the Lord is than who we are.

The greatest elder to give honor to is the Lord Himself.

While we applaud the previous generations, let's continually praise God for revealing Himself through the pillars of the church. We can give honor to the elders, but we must also give the highest honor to the King of kings. He is the God who created all things and is beyond space and time; the One who overcame the grave and pours out His Spirit every day; the One True God whose name is Jesus, whose power exceeds the fiercest oceans. Knowing God is what it's all about! When we see Him for who He has revealed Himself to be, then our influence can bring forth His marvelous light. We can shine our Father's love. The elders of the church are unmovable in their faith because they truly know God for themselves. All their hope is in Jesus, and so they stand. They endure and their legacy will glorify the Lord.

The United States was founded by God-fearing men and women. Their mindset sculpted the culture. Just like the Bible, our nation's history contains many unpleasant memories. Not everything was great or ethical and yet our foundation as a nation knew the Lord. The very basis of all the declarations and laws came from a place of *honoring God.* Our founders didn't do everything right, but they tried and despite their weaknesses and ignorance, the Lord used them anyway to shape our nation.

The world won't stop spinning because we have a testimony, but our testimony can keep the tradition alive of honoring God. When we share our story of who God is and what He's done in our lives, it matters! We aren't required to have the talent of public speaking. We don't need to have eloquent speech or good grammar. The power of influence is a gift and we need to honor the Giver. We are chosen because Jesus uses pillars to hold up other people. He sees our potential to become God-fearing leaders and faithful storytellers.

We're His megaphone of grace to a hurting world.

While the generations before us seem fearless when sharing their stories, fear is crippling ours from being told. It's important to understand the bigger picture concerning the power of influence. We are consumed by doubt and a lack of confidence that we pull back our connection to the truth. We don't feel good enough to share our faith or the testimony of how God changed us. We're allowing other influences to muffle the voices we've been given.

"Herein is our love made perfect, that we may have boldness in the day of judgment: because as he is, so are we in this world. There is no fear in love; but perfect love casteth out fear: because fear hath torment. He that feareth is not made perfect in love."
(1 John 4:17-18)

God wants to be known to the dying beggar, the heartbroken widow and the isolated teenager. Jesus doesn't have to show up, but He does. That's true love. We don't have to be afraid to share our testimonies. God can use it to bring people to Him. He influences society and culture, bringing us back to the basics of faith. When we use our voice to bring forth the messages God wants us to speak, the opportunity for souls to be saved is enhanced.

We've survived trials because God won't give up on us.

The world needs to know about the faithfulness of our Creator. We're afraid to speak about Jesus today as if people will hang us at the gallows, and maybe some might want to, but the reality is most people are searching for answers. Some are actually seeking for a "higher power" but we're too fearful to speak a word. Our nation needs our influence! It doesn't need another lukewarm Christian who thinks more about their outfits on Sunday than bowing to an altar. The world doesn't need another person that looks and acts like they do but secretly believes in God. Our friends don't need another person who won't read their Bible but will anxiously stream live videos on social media at 2am. Our families don't need another person rushing from one thing to the next, numb to the Holy Spirit yet actively aware of to-do lists.

Bravery tells fear that we will serve God anyway.

Our influence won't disappear, so let's be brave. Influence has purpose and God won't strip that away because we're scared. Sharing our story doesn't have to be with a loud roar or raised fists. It can be soft whispers to a friend at lunch, during a family walk around the neighborhood or through email with a curious heart overseas. *You can be brave and afraid.* You're human. If you are willing, God will enable you to share what someone needs. He'll give us the strength regardless of the things we've done and how nervous we are about opening up. God is still moving among His people and His love can never be diminished. Bravery is saying the cross was enough to take care of the darkest sin and Jesus can do it again!

"For God hath not given us the spirit of fear; but of power, and of love, and of a sound mind. Be not thou therefore ashamed of the testimony of our Lord, nor of me his prisoner: but be thou partaker of the afflictions of the gospel according to the power of God; Who hath saved us, and called us with an holy calling, not according to our works, but according to his own purpose and grace, which was given us in Christ Jesus before the world began"
(2 Timothy 1:7-9)

The light of God can't shine forth through a sealed vessel. A covered candle doesn't cast a glow outside of its shell. The same is true for us. Let's not wait anymore. Our lives are a vapor, just a speck on the timeline. How we use this time could change the course of history! There are legacies waiting to be written. What is your legacy going to be? Are you prepared to become a pillar in Christ?

One of the greatest examples for us is in the New Testament. There were many great men and women who shared truth, but one man changed history through sharing his redemption story. He was a powerful leader against God's people but in a quick moment, that all changed.

The added pressure of the chains shackled around his wrists and ankles took his breath away and caused the blood in his veins to pulse with chaos. He slowly walked away. There was a stinging cut above his right eyebrow but it didn't compare to how badly his back was bruised. Warm blood dripped from his nostrils as strong men pushed him towards the door. His feet dragged with every step as the chains chimed a death song. The shouts from the crowd faded away from his ears and an unspeakable peace flooded his countenance.

As the men led him closer to the door, he caught a glimpse of steps that overlooked the crowd. He stopped. A still small voice inside was saying, "Now is the time."

Paul turned towards the guards as he stood amid an angry mob. The people shouted obscene words and they desired to see him destroyed. Turning towards the chief captain, Paul found his voice.

"May I speak with you?" he asked.

After a short discussion with the chief captain, Paul was granted permission to ascend the steps and address the crowd. The crowd of people who wanted him arrested. Paul lifted up his hand and a hush came over the grounds.

(Inspired by Acts 21, KJV)

It was then that Paul spoke about the powerful encounter he had with God while on the road to Damascus. In Acts 22, the crowd is silent as they watch and listen to Paul. Still bound up and arrested, he details his testimony with anointed boldness. He explains how he was once called Saul and had persecuted the Christian people for their faith. That is until the Lord spoke to him.

"And it came to pass, that, as I made my journey, and was come nigh unto Damascus about noon, suddenly there shone from heaven a great light round about me. And I fell unto the ground, and heard a voice saying unto me, Saul, Saul, why persecutest thou me? And I answered, Who art thou, Lord? And he said unto me, I am Jesus of Nazareth, whom thou persecutest. And they that were with me saw indeed the light, and were afraid; but they heard not the voice of him that spake to me. And I said, What shall I do, Lord? And the Lord said unto me, Arise, and go into Damascus; and there it shall be told thee of all things which are appointed for thee to do."
(Acts 22:6-10)

Paul continues to share with the crowd how the Lord used a devoted man named Ananias and through this fellowship, he was delivered. God used an elder to influence Paul and he was converted from an enemy of the Lord to an heir! After this tremendous experience, he took every opportunity to share it with others. That meant laying down fear and speaking to a crowd that didn't like him. It didn't matter that he was wrapped in chains and being held by guards, Paul wanted to talk about God. He desired to touch the hearts of the people with how great he believed God was. Paul was ready to die for sharing his testimony.

"And the night following the Lord stood by him, and said, Be of good cheer, Paul: for as thou hast testified of me in Jerusalem, so must thou bear witness also at Rome."
(Acts 23:11)

Paul's influence changed the world. He understood the power of words and how his influence could make a difference. When he was Saul, his influence was damaging. He was responsible for bringing destruction and death to believers of the Lord Jesus Christ. When God stepped in that day and Saul obeyed His voice, there was a shift. *The influence he had from that moment on brought light and life!* Paul made a choice to obey and follow the Lord. He could no longer could deny the power of God and the revelation he had been given. Paul had to face his own sin head on and turn away from what he thought was right. Paul's new name gave him a new mission and his influence a new purpose.

Saul's influence changed because God changed him.

The fact is, we have influenced someone at some point in time. We probably have today without even thinking about it. Every day we make a choice as to how positive or negative that influence is. It's in our hands. Paul wasn't completely delivered on the spot. He was given a command to find Ananias and follow what the Lord said. *There was action that needed to happen before the miracle.* Fear and distraction are leading us astray and polluting our legacy. Everything is "I want it now and I want it my way." Instant gratification is blurring our vision and the future is hurting because of it.

We need to be modern day Esther's and Paul's. Two different testimonies but one main purpose. They both honored God, spoke boldly in the face of adversity and led wholesome lives no matter what opposition showed up. God preserved their legacy in writing, so others can learn and grow through their stories. Take a minute right now and quietly answer these few questions honestly:

If I stay on the path I'm on, what will my legacy look like?

How will my influence in this life speak of Jesus?

Will I be representing God in the story I leave behind?

How will my present choices affect the future and beyond?

We don't need to know all mysteries to obey God.

All we need is a willing heart that wants to grow in the Lord, according to His Word. *All we really need is more Jesus and less of everything else.* Perhaps, being made in His image means we should be developing His characteristics within us. We shouldn't try to manufacture it by manipulation or pretending. Being more like Jesus happens through the power of the Holy Ghost within us, diligent prayer and studying of the scriptures. This stretches our mindsets to think beyond space and time, so we can have a greater influence in this life.

If you're struggling, look for a pillar. Look for those who are stable and established in the Lord. They are examples for you. They can help redirect your attention back to God. When you look to pillars for guidance, you will get inspired through their influence and that will bring you back to truth.

"But seek ye first the kingdom of God, and his righteousness; and all these things shall be added unto you."
(Matthew 6:33)

This life needs to be more than our daily task lists, dream jobs, college goals and parenting stats. We can't be focused on being well-rounded more than faith-rounded. The Word says to "be like a tree" and that's what I encourage us to be today! Let your knowledge of God be a good, solid foundation and firmly plant yourself. Tap into the Living Water and open yourself to receiving the True Light. Allow yourself to be fed the right nutrients through prayer, Bible reading and living a life of holiness. Be a vessel for good fruit to develop and grow. You will sprout as an energy source and therefore can help nourish others.

Think beyond today and into your future influence.

Isn't the goal to thrive as a Christian and hopefully be used by God to build His Kingdom? It's time we invest in our spiritual future by investing spiritually in the present. This moment is preparation for your position as a pillar in His church. You're not going to be the age you are forever. Time will not stand still for you. Life will go on, the earth will move, people will grow up and things will change. It will be uncomfortable and sometimes messy but that's part of the process. God will always be working, and you will have power to influence the generations to come. Let's start being accountable for it.

Be a pillar, my friend. Strong in the Lord, able to give wise counsel to those who need it. Conduct yourself in a way that glorifies the King. *Be a good difference in a world of wickedness.* Show others an example of a life that sin didn't permanently damage. A heart that sought and found God, whose confidence is in the love of the Lord Jesus Christ. Get in the Throne Room and make an altar. Delete anything in your life that's not drawing you nigh to His water. Break down walls and break free of people that won't help you rebuild. Put up borders of protection and shield yourself from temptation. Learn it's okay to be alone with God and that prayer is never perfect. *Shine like godly glitter, reflecting His character and drawing others closer to His side.*

Living for God will be hard. Just do it anyway.

"For I know the thoughts that I think toward you, saith the LORD, thoughts of peace, and not of evil, to give you an expected end. Then shall ye call upon me, and ye shall go and pray unto me, and I will hearken unto you. And ye shall seek me, and find me, when ye shall search for me with all your heart."
(Jeremiah 29:11-13)

Online References

Appease

https://www.merriam-webster.com/dictionary/appease

Carbon Dioxide

https://www.ccohs.ca/oshanswers/chemicals/chem_profiles/carbon_dioxide.html

Cedar Trees

https://www.gardeningknowhow.com/ornamental/trees/cedar/growing-cedar-trees.htm

Commentary

https://www.biblestudytools.com/commentaries/jamieson-fausset-brown/genesis/genesis-21.html

https://bible.org/seriespage/22-what-happens-when-christians-mess-genesis-211-34

Complete

https://www.merriam-webster.com/dictionary/complete

Crossfire

http://www.dictionary.com/browse/crossfire

Esther

https://womenfromthebook.com/2012/08/14/esthers-make-over-fit-for-a-queen/

Fear

https://www.google.com/search?q=fear+definition&ie=utf-8&oe=utf-8

Fidelity

http://www.dictionary.com/browse/fidelity

Glitter

https://www.collinsdictionary.com/dictionary/english/glitter

https://www.glittermyworld.com/how-glitter-is-made.html

http://tenrandomfacts.com/glitter/

https://en.wikipedia.org/wiki/Glitter

https://www.ibtimes.co.uk/brief-history-glitter-where-it-originated-1647779

https://mineralseducationcoalition.org/minerals-database/mica/

https://www.encyclopedia.com/earth-and-environment/minerals-mining-and-metallurgy/mineralogy-and-crystallography/mica https://wonderopolis.org/wonder/what-makes-glitter-sparkle

Influence

https://www.google.com/search?q=influence+define&ie=utf-8&oe=utf-8

Legacy

https://www.thefreedictionary.com/legacy

Lyrics

http://www.songlyrics.com/hillsong-united/so-will-i-100-billion-x-lyrics/

Media

http://www.the-numbers.com/market/genre/Horror

http://thedailyjournalist.com/pen-and-pad/mass-media-and-its-influence-on-society/

https://www.rand.org/blog/2013/09/what-effect-does-media-have-on-youth.html

https://www.123helpme.com/negative-effects-of-mass-media-on-teenagers-view.asp?id=216323

https://www.ncbi.nlm.nih.gov/pmc/articles/PMC2792691/

https://www.statista.com/topics/842/netflix/

https://expandedramblings.com/index.php/netflix_statistics-facts/

https://www.childtrends.org/wp-content/uploads/2009/05/child_trends-2009_05_26_rb_adolelecmedia.pdf

https://www.medscape.org/viewarticle/569353

https://www.medscape.org/viewarticle/569353

https://www.statista.com/topics/842/netflix/

https://www.statista.com/statistics/250934/quarterly-number-of-netflix-streaming-subscribers-worldwide/

Modesty

http://www.dictionary.com/browse/modesty

Palm Trees

https://en.wikipedia.org/wiki/Arecaceae

Pillar

https://www.merriam-webster.com/dictionary/pillar

Please

https://www.merriam-webster.com/dictionary/please

Prevention

https://www.merriam-webster.com/dictionary/prevention

Quotes

https://www.goodreads.com/author/show/89155.Morton_T_Kelsey

https://www.goodreads.com/quotes/230715-hurt-people-hurt-people-we-are-not-being-judgmental-by

https://quoteinvestigator.com/2014/02/18/stand-fall/

Self-Gratification

https://www.merriam-webster.com/dictionary/self-gratification

Shrapnel

https://www.britannica.com/technology/shrapnel-weaponry

https://todayinsci.com/S/Shrapnel_Henry/ShrapnelHenry.htm

Stagnation

https://en.wikipedia.org/wiki/Water_stagnation

http://biblehub.com/topical/s/stagnant.htm

http://filterbutler.com/blog/standing-water-danger-home/

https://www.restorationlocal.com/restoration-blog/the-dangers-of-stagnant-water/

https://www.ehow.com/info_8558309_stagnant-water.html

Trees

http://www.sciencekids.co.nz/sciencefacts/plants/trees.html

http://canopy.org/tree-info/benefits-of-trees/

https://www.treepeople.org/tree-benefits

http://www.esf.edu/pubprog/brochure/leaves/leaves.htm

Windbreak

https://www.gardeningknowhow.com/ornamental/trees/tgen/windbreaks-in-the-landscape.htm